Friends and Fiddlers

Friends and Fiddlers

By

CATHERINE DRINKER BOWEN

BOSTON

LITTLE, BROWN, AND COMPANY

1945

Published March, 1935
Reprinted July, 1935
Reprinted November, 1935
Reprinted May, 1936
Reprinted May, 1937
Reprinted March, 1939
Reprinted November, 1942
Reprinted May, 1943
Reprinted April, 1944
Reprinted May, 1945

THE ATLANTIC MONTHLY PRESS BOOKS
ARE PUBLISHED BY
LITTLE, BROWN, AND COMPANY
IN ASSOCIATION WITH
THE ATLANTIC MONTHLY COMPANY

PRINTED IN THE UNITED STATES OF AMERICA

To the Sisters

Ernesta and Cecilia Beaux

FOREWORD

SEARCH the library catalogues under "Music," and you will find books on counterpoint, on composers, on Gregorian chants, on the tragedy of Tchaikowsky or the spiritual development of Beethoven. The love letters of Wagner, the compositional difficulties of Brahms, the finest shades of professional musical criticism – all have found their way into print.

But there remains a voice to be heard. Not the voice of your confirmed concert-goer, nor of that fortunate hostess whose music room is graced of an evening by the brilliant concert players of the day, but another voice, modest but none the less insistent. The playing amateur, the hard-bitten fiddler, the string-quartet addict, the piano-duet enthusiast, the lady who cannot sing and knows it, but who forgathers with friends to prove Bach upon the unskillful larynx. These are the people who play for fun and not for audience, the people to whom music is not an "accomplishment," but a daily joy, an abiding comfort. And it is these people, with whom my days have been intimately spent, that I have endeavored to bring to life in a book, to the end that they might prove their musical point to a world which thinks of music in terms unhappily far from intimate.

I am aware that I have, in these pages, confused truth with fiction. To point a musical moral, to adorn a fiddler's tale, I have made straight things crooked, bad men good, and good women as wicked as Eve. From the major protagonists I have already received forgiveness, and for this largesse I make acknowledgment from the bottom of my heart, for nothing is more wounding than a portrait deliberately unjust, and no forgiveness requires a larger nature for the granting.

But to those persons – and experience tells me they will not be few – who may imagine themselves, with angry surety, as Miss Lydia or Miss Mamie, because their names begin with an *L* or an *M*, or because they too wore, one night, a rose in their hair or played a sour note upon their fiddles – to those persons I make my bow and recommend them, for example in the qualities of mercy and serenity, to Victoria and Joe Knoedler and Henry Jones. To Patience, my little Quaker pupil. And especially, with another, deeper bow, to Sarah and to John.

C. D. B.

CONTENTS

Foreword vii

I *Wherein we make our curtsey to music and to our readers, and introduce John, with his coat off, ready to play* 3

II *Background, historic and philosophic, of our family orchestra* 7

III *On musical hunger, its causes and cures* 22

IV *Mæcenas and the muse* 47

V *A friendly art, and some anecdotal proofs of the saying that all quartet players meet sooner or later* . . . 62

VI *Music and marriage, with especial mention of viola wives and of their antithesis* 86

VII *God makes the viola players, but ego makes the soloists* 114

VIII *On cellists, wild and domesticated* . . 131

IX *Family music and roads that lead home to it* 147

Contents

X	*Country music, with an account of Sidney's hospitality and Felicia's, and an introduction to some Gilead choristers*	179
XI	*On organs and organists. Wherein Ernest expounds the true faith, and I explore strange territory*	197
XII	*A little evening of music, or how not to do it*	224
XIII	*And when I shall be old—*	252

Friends and Fiddlers

CHAPTER I

Wherein we make our curtsey to music and to our readers, and introduce John, with his coat off, ready to play

MUSICIANS are fond of saying that music is to be played, not talked about. A professional violinist pronounced this dictum at our house the other night, after he and my brother John had got through a Beethoven sonata. The fact that he played a sonata with John proves Frank Gittelson teacher as well as virtuoso; he spoke with finality. *"Music,"* said he, *"is to be played, not talked about."* A moment later, someone remarked that music, although delightful, was undoubtedly the stupidest, the least taxing mentally, of all the arts. Immediately, Mr. Gittelson laid down his fiddle and was launched into passionate defense, rallying philosophy, psychology, and physics to his aid. For half an hour he talked, eloquently, convincingly, then picked up his fiddle and played again. . . .

To me, one of the most interesting things about

a musician is his personal definition of music. Were I a better violinist than I am, perhaps my instrument would long ago have defined music to my satisfaction; as it is, a life lived intimately with music has made me only the more desirous to shape this intimacy into words; like a lover, I burn to declare myself.

Restless with this desire, yet not daring to approach music with my own words, I sat down before my typewriter and called upon Benet, Schopenhauer, Santayana: "The practice of an art is a satisfaction worn like an amulet against all life's disillusionments." . . . "Art is the quickest way out of Manchester." . . . "Music is the occult metaphysical exercise of a soul not knowing that it philosophizes." . . . "Music is essentially useless, as life is, but both lend utility to their conditions." . . .

For six mornings I called thus upon the wise, and on the seventh I blocked with a penny the key bearing the quotation marks, and sat staring out my window at the poplar trees, heavy-leaved, blowing. . . . And presently I could not see the poplars for the faces crowding. Faces of people who had played music with me, for me; faces of young men with fiddles under their chins; grave faces, shadowed, intent upon the music before them. Faces of children with a violin for the first time in their hands — eager, a little frightened, as though a magic had come to pass under their fingers. People singing, rows of them around me; fat faces, silly faces — but not silly now, because for a little moment they are not themselves, but Johann Sebastian. . . . My mother's face at eighty, rising from the sofa to go upstairs because the "Beethoven *andante* was too strong for her." My brother John at any age, any time, bending over a musical score in his hands; my mother again, nodding across the music room when the gong sounded for dinner, waving a hand to indicate, "You and John may finish the 'Kreutzer,' although you are doing it quite badly, because even bad Beethoven is worth many times hot soup. . . ."

These pictures and many more pass before me, rising with an impact hard and fine; too fine for analysis, too real for sentimentality. I want to write the pictures down; I want it so badly that I know my desire cannot be altogether due to altruism or the urge to help my unmusical neighbor. Something stronger impels me to write, something more personal than a crusade, something nearer to the greedy heart. I know what it is; it is gratitude. I want to write about music because I am grateful. Silly sentiment, gratitude — outmoded, dilute! Nevertheless I am grateful – to music. I am filled with gratitude, heavy with it as those poplar trees are heavy with rain, pulsing with it as their trunks are pulsing with sap; indeed, so richly am I filled that I can even bear your trim quick joke about sap and gratitude. . . .

I cannot illumine these urgent pages with strings of glittering names. No midnight scenes with Gabrilówitsch on my piano stool telling Thibaud to take the *scherzo* a shade faster if he really wants to please the lady. And me upon the divan with a cigarette in my fingers and exactly the right kind of clothes, – something casual in old Venetian brocade, – saying softly, "But, Gabby dear . . ." And everybody happy. Even if I achieved the brocade, I could not wear it because it would get in my fiddle's way. "Roll up your sleeves, ladies," says John. "And take off your coats, gentlemen, before we begin to play. Because after one *allegro,* it will be too late. After one good presto the shirts will be in no condition to be exposed to view." . . . It takes sweat to accomplish even Beethoven Opus 18, Number 1, and as to Brahms. . . . Angry black pages – sixteenth notes, thirty-seconds, sixty-fourths. . . .

CHAPTER II

Background, historic and philosophic, of our family orchestra. Including the earnest and prayerful persuasion of the author against that bogey called Musical Talent

LISTED in the county ledgers as housewife, I have four brothers and a sister, the conventional number of parents, two children, and four nieces and nephews. None of us are professional musicians, and we all live together in a quiet, practical succession of days. But strike A on the piano, blow it on the pitch pipe, and to a man we move to the fiddle cases as mechanically as we move, on occasion, to the telephone bell. People ask us constantly, "Who is responsible for all this music in your households? How has it come to pass?" And they add with a vague look of distress, "We *used* to play the piano, but – "

I cannot bear to hear people say this. It outrages me to see my friends go hungrily to concerts and come away only partially filled – the hunger unappeased, or the appetite whetted, perhaps, to an even keener edge. I know what these people want; I have seen them pick up my violin and turn it over in their hands. They may not know it themselves, but they want music, not by the ticketful, the purseful, but music as it should be had, music at home, a part of daily life, a thing as necessary, as satisfying, as the midday meal. They want to *play*. And they are kept back by the absurd, the mistaken, the wicked notion that in order to play an instrument one must be possessed by that bogey called Talent; one must have been born with specially shaped fingers, have been sprinkled with holy water at birth, or have seen the moon all yellow at the quarter on a Friday night.

To these persons, then, I address myself. In the hazard that I may reveal, not the secret, but the very fact that there is no secret, no mysterious password, no angry gods to be appeased at the portal to the shrine, I offer my musical reminiscences, from the age of seven to thirty-seven. Hastily, in the fear that the words "began to play at seven" may raise again the bogey, I interpolate, before beginning my story, my affidavit that I have seen people begin to play the violin at twenty-seven, the viola at thirty-two, the flute at forty, the cello at sixty-two; not only begin to play, but go on to the essential goal – membership in a hard-playing, musically exacting, weekly-meeting amateur ensemble group.

We are not the descendants of talented musicians. There has never been a professional musician in our family, nor even anyone noted in his community for musical virtuosity. My mother, with only an elementary knowledge of the piano, – she could read hymn tunes and liked to sing the alto part of a Mendelssohn duet, – somehow instilled into my eldest brother, John, a profound passion for music which he in turn communicated to me, sixteen years his junior. Of the four intervening children, the three boys remained immune to music; as a girl my sister Victoria played Mozart with me, played Beethoven too, and then in due course married a musician and began, as she says, to live music instead of abusing it. In defense of my thesis I must add that Victoria is the one person I know who does not need to play music – does not, that is, need it at the moment. At the moment, she is beautiful, active, and triumphant. If ever she may be less of these things, she has music, as it were, up her sleeve; she knows how to play the piano.

When I say the boys remained immune to music, I except such exercises as playing the mandolin in the Glee Club at college, or even the clarinet in the school band. The clarinet is a noble instrument, an instrument of true music; long and mournful its notes when blown from a brother's room in the third story. But when he was grown, my brother abandoned his clarinet. Now he is forty; in the intervals of scientific research he solaces himself upon a four-key harmonica, or even, on occasion, upon a large and complicated piano-accordion.

My children, aged six and nine, accept piano playing and sight singing as they accept breakfast and dinner and the hours that strike round the clock. John's wife and their four children, ranging in age from twelve to nineteen, all play and sing, – and with eagerness, – piano, cello, and violin. String and piano quartets, quintets, octets, choral ensembles, burst into sound at a moment's notice, the difficulty being, not to make the children play, but to keep them from battle when there are not as many parts as musicians.

What interests me in this family music chronicle is the fact that my mother, with so slight a musical knowledge and technique, could have influenced at least two of her children so that music has been the profoundest and happiest fact of their lives, and from all evidence bids fair to have an equal share in the lives of her grandchildren. I deem this worth recording, if only in answer to the many mothers who protest to me, "It 's all very well for you to talk about making music a natural part of children's lives. You and your brother John live next door to each other; you play the violin and he and his wife play the piano; the three of you really know music. Of course you can impart this knowledge and enthusiasm to the six children. But what about the rest of us, who can barely read a hymn tune? How can we direct our children, how can we direct ourselves, along the path of music?"

My mother could barely read a hymn tune herself; my father, who had in his youth sung a very tolerable bass, was, by the time I came to know him, wholly indifferent to music. Indifferent, that is, to the hearing of it; he sponsored music and worked in its behalf. For fifteen years he acted as president of the famous Bach Choir at Bethlehem, accepting the office on condition – so he told us – that he should never be expected to go to a concert. At home, my father endured much in the name of music: a room known as Father's Office was just across the hall from the piano; never once were we told to stop playing. Indeed, my father's patience in the face of overwhelming sound has always been a matter for marvel. I do not remember his ever listening to me play, but he used to encourage me: "Your mother says you are doing very well on your violin." He would have said music was a good thing – good, certainly, for girls. For boys, questionable. He had the attitude of his generation. I suspect his eldest son's piano playing worried my father a little; this intense preoccupation with one of the arts – was it quite the part of a gentleman, of a man of affairs? Not until John became well established as a lawyer did my father's conscience permit him to cease casting small gibes at what he called the "long-hairedness" of music playing.

But what brought music to life in our household and kept it so burningly alive was not my mother's feeble performance upon the piano, not even, I am tempted to believe, her attitude toward music, but a larger thing – her attitude toward art and toward life. Both she and her sister were trained by family environment – in a way curiously indirect – to a respect for the arts, that serious respect which in the end amounts to passionate, yet entirely unassuming, conviction. My Great-Aunt Eliza, my Great-Uncle Will played piano duets, played them *well.* In that household a thing undertaken was a thing finished; there were no loose ends, artistic or practical. My mother and my aunt used to wash the dishes – from necessity, not choice; often enough there was no money for a servant. More than once they have explained to me with pride exactly *how* they washed the dishes. It was a system so perfected as to be almost a ritual; they could, when challenged, clear a table set for five, wash and put away the dishes, have their aprons hung upon the nail and no spot upon the lace cuffs – all in seven and a half minutes. I have heard also how they made the beds and with what care they mended, in the long hot Philadelphia summer days, the hand-woven linen sheets brought down from the attic. And in these recitals is nothing tedious; the sisters tell their story with excitement, with relish, in the same tone they used to tell how the younger sister obtained her first gold medal from the Paris Salon. Dishwashing or portrait painting, high standards were not high to them, because high standards were expected – demanded.

My great-grandmother, who ruled this household, had that type of simplicity which the sixties produced in New England. Art was a thing foreign to her – but refinement was not foreign to her, nor the discipline of mind and character that goes to the creation, the establishment, of good taste. Good taste, in that simple household, was not a social asset, it was a matter of morals, of what people used to call "character"; it consisted in perfecting to the best of one's ability what one had undertaken to do or to learn or to make. To these children, perfection was no bogey, no nightmare; by their own account it was a house filled with laughter and gayety. Yet I am constantly amazed at the hints which slip from my mother concerning the enormous things which were expected, as a matter of course, from her and her sister. They learned a habit of Perfection – and with it bound themselves forever to Perfection's sister, the dangerous but fascinating habit of Intensity. My mother is eighty; she has never been a stern woman, – her laugh is high and quick, like a girl's, – but to this day she flies at a task as if the witches were after her, and she expects others to do the same. With stupid people she has patience, but lazy people are beyond her comprehension; she hears of them in astonishment, as though she were hearing of a baboon, something existent but not quite human.

I will not make the boast that my great-grandmother's spirit has come down undiluted to me and my brothers and our children. I will not try to argue that, as a family without talent, we achieved music through "character." But I must pause to give tribute to the much maligned Puritan discipline. The stern fanatic eye which said, "Do with all thy heart that to which thou has set thy hand" – that was a hard eye to meet. But, if met, how glorious the reward! I remember well my mother's words when, at seven, I told her I wanted to play the violin. She took my hands and looked at me. "That is not an easy thing to do," she said. "It will take courage. Do you think you will be up to it?"

Up to it! Years passed before I understood the full meaning of her words; at that moment I did not need to understand them. What child would not have risen to such a challenge? Flags waved, banners flew. But I know now why she used the word "courage." For without courage no one can be a sincere artist, even an amateur artist. Ridicule pursues the aspiring fiddler. One of the best violinists I know told me that when she began to play, the neighbors' children – among them her bosom friend – gathered under the window daily and shouted *"Meow!"* – shouted it tirelessly, enthusiastically, until her practice time was over. Children to whom music is unfamiliar look upon violin-playing children with a combination of curiosity, ridicule, and that grudging, instinctive respect which even your adult "practical man" grants an artist.

But I care not how the world looks upon music, if only the world be not indifferent to it. "To music," says the philosopher, "we must remain inattentive altogether or become altogether enslaved."

And we who are enslaved, to what quality of this art of music do we owe the strength, the glory, of our chains? What is this close, this hungry relationship between music and life? I know of one answer, at least; of one quality music, alone among the arts, possesses – a warm, a satisfying friendliness. All the other arts are lonely. We paint alone – *my* picture, *my* interpretation of the sky. *My* poem, *my* novel. But in music – ensemble music, not soloism – we share. No altruism this, for we receive tenfold what we give. Our fiddle bow draws out high C; gives it out, thin and true and long, to three other fiddlers under the lamp. And back it comes, realized, made authentic by the viola G, the clean, the vigorous fifth, softened by the second violin's E flat, – pleasant, drowsy minor interval! – strengthened now by the cello's deep, tonic C, the full chesty burr of his open string. The chord dies; and the four of you sit silent, smiling. The first fiddler nods. "Not so bad," he says. "Not – so – bad."

Perhaps it is this warm yet impersonal friendliness of music that causes people to look so wistfully upon our family quintets, our neighborly octets. Certainly I never saw that nostalgic envy creep into the eye of anyone listening to a piano solo. *Ensemble,* that is the key to musical enjoyment. Your soloist, no matter how skillful, is a bird of different feather, and your concert-goer, though he feed upon symphony as a lamb upon milk, is no true lover if he play no instrument. Your true lover does more than admire the muse; he sweats a little in her service.

An instant flash, an instant communication, passes between strangers who discover a mutual love of ensemble playing. Perhaps this same communication is established between mutually discovered bridge players, between fishermen. I do not know, but I know the reality of this other, the warm invisible bond, the banishment of aloneness, the sudden reawakening, reawareness of life, that only communication brings. To break for an instant that shell, that hard protection with which every adult surrounds himself – what glorious, delicious indulgence! And to know it broken, not in dissipation, – as in any vulgar, too easy effort at communication, – but broken with the brain sharp, the eye clear, the ear alert, and the belly hot with triumph. . . .

Sometimes, driving home after an evening of quartets, the thought has come to me: Suppose the Lord had made me, let us say, a tennis maniac instead of a melomaniac. A few years, and I shall be forty – pushed off the court! No wonder people fall into panics concerning old age. But with music, one's pleasure, one's participation, grows rather than diminishes with the years. Not only are new beauties discovered, new loves introduced, but new meaning is revealed in the old love! Beethoven, for instance. When I was young I loved Beethoven because I loved the tunes, the melody; as a child I had been literally rocked to sleep to the "Kreutzer Sonata": John and the old Steinway – not old, then – fighting it out in the parlor below until my small white iron bed shivered and my spine shivered with it. John was getting ready for Katrina, who would come down from Boston with her violin next month or next week-end; Katrina was an excellent violinist. A formidable alliance, Katrina and Beethoven, for a young lawyer to attempt to enter; no wonder the walls shook and the ceiling of the old parlor rocked to six-eight time! John practised the "Kreutzer" like one demented; whistling the violin parts, he practised it at night and he practised it before breakfast, and it will haunt me till I die – but I am not sorry. Indeed, it was the "Kreutzer" that was responsible for the commencement of my fiddling career; I remember well my amazement when Katrina, arriving, took out her fiddle, nodded to John – and did things to the "Kreutzer." Magic things: what was this wild, slippery voice creeping in and out, so deep, so high, so like John's "Kreutzer" and yet so more-than-John?

So it was *this* John had meant when he had said, "Wait till you hear the fiddle! Wait till you hear the two of us!" And now I was hearing it. I sat on the red parlor sofa with my mother; I remember my legs dangling, the pressure of my mother's hand around my fingers and her quick smile answering mine. I whispered, "What *is* it, Mother?" She said, "It 's Beethoven, child" – and I was a little offended that she could have thought me so stupid. But I know now that she could not more richly have answered my bewildered question. When they had done I went to John and told him solemnly that I wanted to do that, too, and he laughed his great laugh of pleasure. I remember his hand upon my shoulder and his face upturned to Katrina, – whom I remember not at all, – his eager voice, "Do you think the Infant could do it?"

For years I practised with the "Kreutzer" as goal; I am grateful to John that he never hinted at its difficulties, its impossibilities, though he more than once hinted at the difficulties of violin technique. "You can't fool with a fiddle," he told me. "It means *work*" – and he made me, upon my mother's advice, promise two years of piano lessons before I ever touched a violin. "To see if you really mean it, Infant." I served my two years' bondage and I had my reward; indeed, I have been having it ever since!

But Beethoven – Beethoven was magic to me then, Beethoven was melody, swinging, rushing melody, music like a thunderstorm. And indeed I remember, years later, running through the hall in a thunderstorm with John and Beethoven matching it out in the parlor through the open door. . . .

Beethoven is not a thunderstorm to me now; he speaks to my maturity with a voice more quiet, yet more triumphant, than the thunder. He has walked through the thunder and has come out unscathed. It would be an impudence and a vanity for me to attempt to put upon paper what Beethoven is to me now. Nothing can say it save the music itself. . . . Thus far, Santayana was right: "Music is not a criticism of violins, but a playing upon them."

But I wonder, when I shall be old, what Beethoven will have in store for me? What further, deeper reaches of beauty, what revelation of hours serenely lived?

CHAPTER III

On musical hunger, its causes and cures, together with some of the author's cherished prejudices and an exposition of various defensive attitudes, into which the truly musical are pushed

WE were playing quartets, upon a Tuesday night at the house of Dr. Retinus, as is our custom, and Joe Knoedler, as is his custom, had brought a girl. On this particular evening, when the quartet was ended, the girl asked a polite question about music – a natural question and innocent enough, yet received by Joe in scorn and astonishment, as though she had questioned the validity of his existence.

Joe Knoedler is our viola player – the best player, incidentally, in the quartet. He is a tall, dark young man, by profession a bridge builder; upon the fiddle he is what athletes call a "natural." He seldom practises and I am inclined to believe that when he sits down to play he automatically places his intelligence on the shelf, for fear it will get in his way. But by instinct or by some dark collusion with the angels, Joe Knoedler, whether the piece be strange to him or familiar, knows the proper tempo, he knows where a phrase begins and where it ends; under his perfect emphasis the dead notes group themselves and spring to life. Impatiently, while he plays, he shouts at the three of us: "Wrong! You are playing it wrong." But when we put down our fiddles and ask him what is wrong, he is speechless. He blushes. "I can't *tell* you," he mutters. "But I can *play* it for you. Here – listen."

But with his girls Joe's technique is at the same time more predictable and less inspired. "Dr. Retinus," he says, "Mrs. Bowen, Mr. Jones – meet Miss Delilah" – and he puts the girl in a chair with a book and tells her to stay there. This particular girl behaved, we all thought, remarkably well; for two hours she had not spoken a word. At the end of that time Joe Knoedler laid down his viola, got to his feet, and shook his great shoulders like a dog coming out of the water. He heaved a vast sigh, lit a cigarette, and stood dazed and speechless. It was now that his girl broke silence.

"Joe," she said brightly, "you certainly do enjoy the music, don't you?"

Joe did not hear her. His face was flushed; he had sat down again and was polishing the viola with a large yellow handkerchief. It is John's viola – a rare and glorious instrument – and Joe, from Tuesday to Tuesday, is very jealous of it. If I bring it to quartets with a speck of rosin under the bridge, he frowns. "What slapstick fiddler has been fooling with my instrument?"

His girl watched him as he turned the viola in his hands. "Joe!" she repeated, louder this time. "You certainly do enjoy playing music, don't you?"

"En*joy* it?" Had she asked him, "Do you enjoy that curious recurrent throb that takes place above four thousand times an hour just under your third left rib?" Joe could not have been more surprised. He got up. "I don't stop to think about enjoying quartets. I don't stop to think about enjoying music anyway." He wheeled and flung his cigarette into the fire. "I got to have music, that 's all," he said with surprising violence. "I just got to have it."

"It appears that a distinct appetite, different from hunger or the sexual appetite, is satisfied by works of art, and the satisfaction of this appetite is a source of pleasure greatly valued by its possessors. This appetite has never been properly investigated. We know practically nothing about its physiological conditions, and as little about its evolution. It may even be that it is confined wholly to man, although authorities differ on this point."

Like almost everything that has been written about æsthetics, this paragraph of J. W. N. Sullivan's is pure speculation. To ask the unmusical to believe in a definite musical hunger is like asking the unbeliever to pray for rain. Keats said he had to prove things "upon his pulses." Women possess a strong social instinct; they prove things, often enough, upon somebody else's pulses. Sullivan called the satisfaction of artistic appetite a "source of pleasure," an insidious understatement which I am glad to disprove upon Joe Knoedler's pulses. To sit down at table is a pleasure – but it is not for pleasure's sake one seeks food. Granted that æsthetic hunger is not one of the primary appetites, and that the need for art does not appear until the belly is filled; granted that a string quartet is a highly civilized affair – then grant also that, without art, civilized man would perish. To say that art saves him would be as illogical as to say the feet are there to save the nose from many a hard bump on the ground; what I say is that man needs art, needs it fiercely, insistently, repeatedly, the way he needs food. Art is exciting and man craves excitement – seeks it, sometimes, even to the gallows' foot. If he be lucky, he finds it in love, or he finds it flying upside down in a Fokker. But love is short and Fokkers crack up. Joe Knoedler finds his excitement in music.

It is an old story, the power of music – music that can drive men to war, to love, to God. According to each man's essence is the direction thereof – and the definition. Sometimes it does not drive at all, but lays hands upon the troubled spirit, to soothe and to heal. Music has done that for me; all my life, music has been healer. As such it has never failed me, or I remember no such failure. When I was young, at unhappy moments I fled to the hills, to the woods, and found my comfort there; but now, in my middle years, it needs stronger enchantment to exorcise the demon, a message more urgent than the gentle melancholy of the wind, the far, quiet pattern of clouds against a high horizon. I hate to suffer this defeat at the hands of my old friends; I am impatient, then, with the wooded dark hills, the gentle meadows. I cry out to them, and they do not respond. They lie dead; their name is scenery. . . .

But music – music never took a name and failed me. Music speaks, and I reply. Slowly my cold blood warms; in my veins I feel it swell and quicken. Once more the heart leaps eagerly, once more I am blinded with the glory that surrounds me.

If in middle life I turn consciously to music as physician, as a child the need was as great and the instinctive turn to music as quick; but the healing was not, I suspect, so much a matter of æsthetic satisfaction as pride of skill, joy of increasing control. Fiddle playing was my compensation – I confess it with current psychological phrases snapping at my heels – my compensation for a chin too long, a forehead too high. I had a beautiful older sister; I have her now, to my joy and pleasure; but she was not always my joy and pleasure. She was something more important; she was spur to my pride, whip to my ambition. That wide brow from which the dark hair swept in bold perfection, the nobly modeled, delicate curve of chin, the tapering fingers – artists, looking at Victoria, drew in the breath. Other men than artists fell in love with her, fell in rows, like ninepins. It was the family joke: "Who 's coming, over Sunday?" "Oh, Victoria's Alec," or "Victoria's Tom." And then, from my brother John: "It 's all right, Infant. They 're not allowed in the parlor."

In the parlor was the piano. With my fiddle under my chin, I too would have a lover. Lovers. Haydn, at first. Jolly, frank Papa Haydn, and

Mozart, when my fingers grew more facile. What if, at parties, boys called me a good sport, instead of *pretty?* In the parlor was my refuge, in the parlor was something more powerful – I knew this in my heart – more powerful, if I but mastered it, than line of brow and line of chin.

I would never be pretty because my bones were all wrong. It needed no measuring tape to tell me; I had heard enough talk concerning other people's very right bones ever to mistake, beneath my own skin or another's, a right bone from a wrong one. One summer day when my aunt was in Europe, two ladies came to see her portraits; one was an artist and one was Cousin X, a dimly distant relative whom I have not seen since that far afternoon. Their voices drifted to me where I sat reading on the verandah.

"Glorious painting," said the first lady. "Is this *all* the family?"

Cousin X replied that no, there was another girl, the youngest, but she had never been painted. About eleven years old. An intelligent child, but not, you know, paintable. "Not a forehead to paint," said Cousin X. "When I saw her in the cradle I remember telling her mother, *'There's* a forehead that will go to Bryn Mawr and write a *book!'* "

To Bryn Mawr and write a book. To Bryn Mawr! Rage filled me; rage burned to my finger tips and drove me indoors, that afternoon, to the parlor. To the cheap fiddle case under the old sofa and the brown magic that lay therein. Never, never to Bryn Mawr! I swore it, kneeling against the sofa. Never to any of their stuffy colleges, to be a spinster with a forehead and her skirts hanging wrong. I would play the violin. I would work and work until I could play like Kreisler, like *two* Kreislers; until I could play better – ten thousand times better – than any of them painted. What if they did paint kings and princes, and were paid for it? I would play for kings and princes, and they would pay *me.*

I never went to Bryn Mawr, and certainly I never played for kings and princes! I went through school failing at mathematics because I took time out to practise my violin; at eighteen I slammed the school door behind me and entered the Peabody Conservatory in Baltimore – achieving the Conservatory, however, not without struggle. At boarding school near Baltimore my music teacher was Van Hulsteyn; he it was who fortified me in my swift and desperate attack, that last term in school, against the Bryn Mawr cohorts. I remember my father's quiet warning, when at John's intercession he agreed to let me "go on with my music." "I want you to keep your balance, child," he said, "and to remember that with us music is an accomplishment, not a profession."

A gauntlet thrown, could my father but have known it; no direct challenge could have struck swifter fire to my tinder. I was too ignorant of the world of real music to know that eighteen is far too old to begin serious musical preparation for a professional life. But for four years, the duration of a college course, I worked at music, and what I learned I did not learn easily. I had little natural ability for music; compared with the pale, black-haired youths about me, I was a mere ignoramus, dull-eared, slow-witted – and the youths did not hesitate to let me know it. "Why are you here?" they would ask me, their lips turned out in scorn, and the question filled me, not with humiliation or any doubt, but with triumph and the sound of wings.

My training, while it had been sound enough as to violin technique, had been old-fashioned, omitting all sight singing, ear training, and harmony. To my chagrin I found I could not, except upon paper, distinguish major from minor; as to a diminished seventh, I had never heard of it. My first orchestra practice was a nightmare. The music before me looked easy – four or five notes to the measure. But when Strube raised his baton and my bow touched the strings, a blare of brasses arose and deafened me into unconsciousness. I was lost completely. I sat there trembling, my fiddle on my knee. Morning after morning this happened. "Put your fiddle in the oven and burn it, Gott-forsaken amateur!" Strube shouted, pointing at me with his baton. He was a little round man with thick glasses, a fierce, intelligent expression, and a voice that on occasion roared like a wounded elephant; he had but to glance in my direction to reduce me to utter helplessness.

The second semester I was, to my surprise, moved up to the first stand among the second violins. At home that summer John helped me with rhythm, patiently teaching me to count out loud while I played – a habit that in later years has stood me in good stead. The following autumn I was delighted and a little terrified to find myself at the first orchestra stand with the *Concertmeister,* one Isaac Bernheimer. Isaac was twenty-three; he was an excellent violinist, studying for a Master's diploma; in the evenings he was to be found leading the dance orchestra at the Hotel Belvidere. When I sat down beside him he nodded briefly, told me my violin was no good and my bow was no good, and asked me if I wanted to buy new ones. He knew, he said, where they were to be had.

Strube, I think, must have put me at the first stand merely because I tried so hard. Certainly he had no illusions about my virtuosity. It was a case of "Be good, sweet maid, and let who will be clever." I was still a God-forsaken amateur, but I never missed a rehearsal, and, once seated on the platform, I never took my eyes off the conductor (a trick which my own subsequent experience in leading vague-eyed choruses has taught me will seduce any conductor).

"Why do you work so hard?" Isaac asked me one morning. "You can run all day and all night, but you will never catch up to me. You are not poor. Why do you work so hard?"

"I like it," I told him. What else could I say? My eye was on no goal; a week at the Conservatory had sufficed to blot forever the vision of myself as a second Kreisler, or indeed a second anything, except a second fiddle. I knew only that, as drop by drop I devoured knowledge of music, I was assuaging a lifelong thirst. I was filled with a profound, a fervent satisfaction.

For me at last the sincere milk of the word! No wonder I was satisfied, have continued satisfied my life long whenever I have opened my throat to that everlasting warmth. And for this, whom shall I thank? How easy to have lived when man gave votive offerings to his god! I should like to fill my pitcher with wine, my cruse with oil; I would walk the path to music's temple, and the way would be very pleasant to me. It would ease my heart to pour the wine, the oil, upon that altar. And yet – in that day of votive offerings were no violins. Mozart had not lived and died; the Lord God Jehovah had not yet found his Name, that name to which Johann Sebastian was to lift up a song of praise as mighty, as immortal, perhaps, as the Name itself. . . . Four fiddles under a lamp – this voice of eloquence called a string quartet was only a zither then, a lute. I am well content, therefore, looking upon my violin, to give thanks less beautifully but no less heartily by the testimony of pen and ink.

For years, all unconsciously, I did this very thing. For years every page I wrote contained some transcription, some expression of my *confessio fidei musicalis.* These published testimonials did me more harm than good. Editors frowned at me: "That was a good story, but why bring music into it?"

How could I keep music out of it? The first publisher I ever met quashed me flat with this kind of indictment. He had turned down a manuscript of mine, a novel with the traditional plot of art versus domesticity; he said he wanted to see me, and on a hottest August day I crept downtown on a trolley and was ushered into his sanctum. Because he was the first publisher I had ever met, I was shy and frightened and wore, to bolster me up, my best Paris dress, given me by Victoria, and gloves. When I came in, the publisher and his cigar were seated behind a big desk; they remained seated. I stood up, and I still think this gave the publisher an unfair advantage; also, he was coatless, tieless, with no gloves on. All the same, he was fatter than I by a stone and he must have been fully as hot – I hope so. Anyway his forehead simmered visibly.

He said, "Well-Mrs.-Bowen-I-read-your-book-three-months-ago-and-I'm-not-going-to-publish-it-but-I-remember-it-very-well-there's-entirely-too-much-music-in-it-have-you-written-another?"

At this time I did not know how publishers talked; I did not know that to a publisher, as to other men, business is – and quite properly – business. I said, "Oh!" – and it sounded inadequate, not at all the way an author should sound talking to a publisher, so I took off my gloves and shifted from the right foot to the left (all fiddlers stand on the left foot to give the bow arm more freedom) and said feebly: –

"Too much music? But that 's what the novel is *about!* It 's about music."

This publisher had an extraordinary facility with a cigar. With both hands occupied at the desk he could, merely by moving the muscles of his lips, shift a cigar from the left side of the mouth to the right. He did it now. He said: –

"Oh, you put all that music in just for effect! You wanted to show off how much you know about music." And while the blood roared in my ears he reached for the telephone on his desk, barked a number, and was hurling insults at an author uptown. He said, "Listen, Mr. Blank, perhaps you 'll make two hundred dollars on this book, but I doubt it. Listen, that dirty joke you took two and a half pages to tell, you should have got it all in one paragraph. . . . *Yeah?"* – and shut off the telephone and glared at me, up and down, Paris dress and all. He said: –

"Are you really going to write any more books, Mrs. Bowen? What do you do for a living, or don't you work?"

I said, *"Certainly,* I 'm going to write more books, and I 'm a music teacher."

(I was not a music teacher, but only yesterday

John had asked me if I would teach his youngest child to play the violin.) And then I said, very sweetly, "There 's just one thing I 'd like to ask you, Mr. Linotype." And when he asked, "What 's that?" I said, "How do I get back where I came from?"

I still burn, three years later, with unsaid replies to this publisher, with unuttered repartee and insults unflung. When he said, "You put in all that music to show off," I should have said – I should have said . . .

Anyway, the novel was published. The man that published it – and in the publishing world his name is Solon – told me, "What I like about your book, Mrs. Bowen, is the very genuine way you let music run all through it."

But Mr. Linotype – alas for revenge – will never know what Solon said, because, even if Mr. Linotype chanced to see this article, he would not read it. There is too much music in it.

Nevertheless, after that I was more careful. In a story where the heroine and the villain fell in love while playing string quartets, on first writing I permitted the villain this: "We 'll play the 'F Major,' darling," said Desmond, "Opus 59." I changed it to read, "the Beethoven with the grand *adagio,*" and then I remembered that publisher and took out the name of Beethoven and the term *adagio,* although my lip curled in self-scorn as I made the erasure and I thought, "Why is America reared to look upon good music as bluestocking?" But, being in need of immediate sales, I caused Desmond to say, "Get out your fiddles; we 'll play a classical quartet" – which turned my blood quite cold with embarrassment, the word *classical,* misused, being to a musician what the word *hand-painted* is to a painter.

But, although I have no patience with people who decry good music as bluestocking, I understand a little the origin of their discomfort in the presence of music's high priests and priestesses. None of the arts is more widely abused by the æsthetic *poseur.* While your musical *poseur* is instantly detected by a musician and ignored with a sigh and a shrug, he cannot be exposed by a person ignorant of music. Hence your unmusical person of intellectual honesty goes about scowling and putting up the lip at every amateur who professes enthusiasm for music not made by Victor Herbert.

I knew a college professor who fell into fury at the name of Mozart. "Motesart, Motesart!" he would mutter. "Why can't you call him Moseart like a good American?" It must have been sheer perversity—for he was an educated man—that prompted him always to speak of a sonat*o* and a concert*a*. This man had the strangest attitude toward music. He scorned it, and said so with a really amusing eloquence, but he went stubbornly to symphony concerts, and when he got there he always fell asleep. He was an excessively nervous man, high-strung; I have seen him sleep through the Tchaikowsky "Pathétique," cymbals and all, and come away smiling. Once I saw him, the day after such a sleeping symphony, sleep all morning on the sunny terrace opening off John's music room while John and some other enthusiast banged away at two-piano duets with every door and window wide. I never could persuade this man to give music credit for easing the taut pegs of his nerves; a tom-tom, he declared, would do as well, not only for him, but for all of us, and the only reason he paid for symphony tickets was because none of his friends possessed a tom-tom.

Your genuine musician gives to ignorance fairer treatment than ignorance gives to him; perhaps this is a mere truism, a comparison of wisdom's tolerance with the fool's impatience. Your musician is always hoping, hoping to find yet another enthusiast, and he will listen patiently to much nonsensical flattery on the chance that it is mere embarrassment covering up a genuine appreciation. On the other hand, I often wish musicians would be a little less patient.

Once a professional string quartet was engaged for an evening of music at a private house of enormous wealth. They played in a huge, stone-walled, stone-floored room hung with tapestry and carpeted with priceless rugs – the worst room, acoustically, I have ever experienced. I was in the front row, but even here the notes fell muffled, as though the place were lined with velvet. At rehearsal the cellist, casting about desperately for some means of relief, removed the rug from under the musicians' four chairs, rolled it up, and asked a servant to dispose of it. The night of the concert the rug was back again, and, the lady of the house being busy with several hundred guests, our cellist sought her social secretary and requested that the rug be removed, explaining patiently that nobody could hear the music with it down. The secretary said briefly, "Mrs. de Smythe knows how music should be arranged in her house," and the rug stayed where it was.

Now, in the name of toil and its reward, in the name of money paid and service rendered, should the musicians have submitted to this? Who was I to judge this complicated question of social economy – I, an amateur, sitting in the front row with my green velvet bosom heaving in rage?

Strange, indeed, the crimes which are committed against music. One pleasant result of that evening's atrocity against Schubert – for it was Schubert over whose singing mouth Madame Secretary had clapped her hand – one pleasant result was that when the party was over, and the lobster-champagne consumed, we repaired, half a dozen congenial souls and the musicians, to the cellist's house and had some music. We had the Brahms "Piano Quintet" and then we had Viennese waltzes, whirling solemnly round and round in couples, the musicians, their fiddles under their chins, circling among us, grinning delight at their own gypsy slides up and down the fingerboard.

Only the true musician knows how to take music seriously enough to be able to take it lightly. If prayer is an art, so is flirtation: only your true artist, to whom music is a thing serious as his own life – only he knows how to flirt with music, to follow up a Bach fugue with a café waltz and derive, as it were, equal pleasure from both. The giant can afford to laugh at Lilliput; perversely enough, it is more often the pygmy who is heard cracking jokes at the giant. Strong men are notoriously good-natured, as are the wise. As for me, I am neither strong nor wise, and my performance on the violin is so unequal to my passion for that instrument as to make the gods themselves laugh.

Nevertheless I have worked hard and joyfully in the service of music; I shall go on working, and this gives me, I think, the privilege of airing a grievance, of listing with emphasis – perhaps with venom – certain things I wish, musically speaking, that people would not say to me.

The actual number of these remarks seems, happily, to diminish with years. Nobody sighs to me, nowadays, "Oh, *please* play 'Humoresque' – you know, the one that goes *dum, de dum, de dum de dum!*" And it is seldom I endure the familiar coo, "You do *love* your violin, don't you?" I thought I was rid of the bird remark, too, and then at one of John's singing parties it came sourly back to me. With windows wide to June we had been singing, some hundred strong, the Brahms "Requiem" – had, indeed, just ended the tuneful chorus, "How lovely is thy dwelling place." We paused, and while the slow heavenly refrain still hung upon the air a robin called from the garden and my most cherished friend, my pal, my crony, turned from the music in her hand and said dreamily, "All the same, that bird can beat Brahms hollow."

What is this eternal, idiotic argument of art versus nature? Why do people think they have to stand up for the bird? I wish I could infect one of these bird provers with an aphasic toxin which would cause her to forget utterly the sound of a violin, rendering unrecognizable the sound of bow on catgut. Then I would sit in a tree outside her window and waken her, some May morning, to the first measures of Beethoven's "Spring Sonata." Especially I should like to try this experiment upon the latest offender – a writer who spends her days, not appreciating nature, but outwitting nature, outspeaking, outheralding the bird. How avidly she would reach for her notebook and the pencil under her pillow, and with what eloquence she would write of the miracle she had discovered! A bird with throat more liquid than the nightingale, with deeper bell-tone than the thrush.

The bird remark is not intrinsically wicked; it is never made except by persons who cannot read music, and it is spoken idly, without malice aforethought. It is a species of sigh, an explosion of the breath – a defense, perhaps, against unpleasant sensations of ignorance or against capture by the music that has been played. "I am slipping, I lose myself, I smother under this new thing. Quickly, quickly let me deny this beauty and save myself! . . . Beethoven? – *Ah, but that bird can beat Beethoven at his own game.*"

But there is another remark more deadly by far, and not so amiable of analysis. Not a week passes without its being breathed in my ear; even now, at the ten-thousandth hearing, my teeth grit in my jaw: –

"I adore music, but I don't know a note."

A letter containing this remark came to me only yesterday from a woman who has earned a brilliant worldly success in her chosen artistic field. And so, madam, you adore music? Lady, lady, you lie in your teeth! You who know ambition, who know hard work, and who through hard work have learned that artistic appreciation is not to be had for the asking, how dare you so confidently approach the throne? Now Pan, God of the Reed, now Memnon, Son of Morning, I adore thee – but I have never troubled to learn the simplest rites of thy ceremonial altar, the simplest song with which to worship thee. Boldly I approach the sacred fire, loudly I acclaim its divine heat. . . . You? Why, lady, you can't even play a mouth organ. You don't know – it is your boast that you don't know – the notes of the musical staff. You adore English literature, too, but I observe that you took time to learn to read. You adore gardens – and you found out long ago which plants come up in May and which lie hidden until September.

An hour after I had read this woman's letter I went to a party, and a painter came up and began telling about an exhibition of modernistic paintings that had just opened in the B— Galleries. The man was not only a good painter, he was a good talker. What an exhibition of modernistic paintings means to me is tired feet dragging exhausted backbone through mile after mile of bleak rooms lined with flat, gaudy-colored symbols of something incomprehensible; under the painter's spell this prospect became golden, lightsome, and desirable. I was keyed to the very mood: *I adore pictures, but* –

"Will you," the painter was saying, "go with me to the exhibition?"

This man did not want to pilot me through an exhibition any more than he wanted to roll an egg through it with his teeth; he wanted at the moment to talk about what he loved, and I was the nearest person. Just in time something came to my rescue, something entirely outside and beyond me. I heard my voice, firm and loud, saying,

"I only like pictures one at a time, and sitting down."

The painter stared, then he blew out his breath in a whistle. "What a relief," he said. "What a relief!"

My declaration had been stupid; it was like the professor and the tom-tom; deliberately I was permitting my ignorance to bar me from the delight, the excitement of exploration in a new field. I know also that in his heart the painter was sad because someone – no matter who – had denied his god. But a good loud denial, a hearty curse, has in it the seed, the very virus, of future affirmation. It may lead to something; it possesses, at any rate, more virtue than the weedy gush of insincerity. With me, that day, denial had its birth in horror lest I approach a serious thing too easily, with too cheap a familiarity – *I adore music, but I don't know a note.*

Must Apollo, then, be clapped upon the back, and Rotarian fellow feeling be proclaimed? Is not love compounded also of respect, or is the word outmoded? To me, at least, respect is the heart, the very essence, of passion. The difficulty is that respect, once admitted, takes up so much room in the mansion that is ourselves. Cluttered with the proud furniture of worldly affairs, with goings and comings and givings and takings, what place remains for humility, for the reception of that guest who visits only the meek? The habitation of the pure in heart – what disciplined sweepings, what sacrificial storages, have made it ready for the high company it may receive! *The pure in heart,* we are told, *shall see God.* And, by that same token, thrice blessed are the pure in heart because, when the fiddles are tuned, they can truly hear the "Fifth Symphony"!

CHAPTER IV

Mæcenas and the muse. The Izzies and the Edwards, or, pride sours the fiddle string

I WENT, in the middle of January, to a stylish Musical Evening. Victoria conducted me, Victoria in Poiret brocade with silvered Poiret laurel leaves about her hair. And indeed I was glad to go, for a famous string quartet waited at the north end of this ride. As the taxi approached Park Avenue, Victoria caviled at my use of the word "stylish." "Why you should assume," she said indignantly, turning upon me a wide perfect brow under Poiret laurels, "why you should assume that merely because people have money, they know nothing about music, or about art, or life, or any of those large angry things . . ."

"Because they don't, darling," said Victoria's husband suddenly, surprisingly, from the other taxi corner.

Victoria raised long white hands from a furred Chanel lap. "But then," she protested, "what is the use of the best education, and being surrounded always with beautiful things, and moving about the world to see the world – what is the use of cultivation and refinement if it only blinds one? I don't believe it," she said indignantly. "Kate, you are posing, and you, Larry, are simply being disloyal to your kind." She flashed upon her husband bright, glorious dark eyes. "You 've money yourself, Larry. You 've always had it. And," she added triumphantly, "*you* write music."

Larry took off his silk hat, looked into it, and put it on again. "Not," he said quietly, "the best music."

It has puzzled me for long, this question of wealth versus artistic achievement. For long I denied the existence of such an antagonism, asking myself: Because I am poor, must I then be a poverty snob? Your self-made man, though he be rich as Crœsus, is not, unless he wishes it, outlawed from real musical participation. He knows how to put his hand and heart to labor, he knows how to throw himself into things; above all, it is his habit to risk failure. It is your child of wealth that suffers. How many great composers were born rich? I do not know the answer; perhaps your child of wealth, recognizing early the power that is his, does not need the consolation, the compensation, of music.

Only later, when he glimpses the appalling chasm that lies beneath him, he turns desperately to art – but it is, for him, too late. He must rest content with the status of connoisseur. He can collect rare fiddles, he can finance a string quartet – and, God be praised, he does it. But he cannot learn, in his fortieth year, to play the cello, as I have seen a humbler man learn. In spite of himself, he thinks it is a little beneath him: Crœsus, son of Crœsus, with a cello between his knees? Never! And for the sins of his fathers, he forfeits thus the Kingdom of Heaven. . . .

Again, it is a question of values, of how much respect is due to art, how much passion the goddess requires of her initiate before she will accept him as disciple. I had an argument about this, not long ago, with Amanda. Amanda is a mother, rich, intelligent, well-bred, and the argument – call it rather the encounter, for little was said – took place after I had chaperoned Amanda's child to her music lesson.

Why, at fifteen, Patricia needed chaperonage, it was not for me to ask; I was content with the privilege, for she learned from a most eminent master. We were driven to town by a chauffeur, Patricia remarking as we left the Park that we were late but, Oh, well, little Izzy would n't care. Little Izzy turned out to be not so small as slight, with the smooth pallor of his race, a fiery dark eye, and a nervous restlessness of motion which changed to strength the instant he put violin to shoulder. The lesson was held upstairs in a room lined with rusty panels stained, apparently, with shoe blacking. Gauze curtains, baby blue, hung grimly at the windows; an empty fireplace, a mantel garnished with horrible glass vases, – ten-cent green ones, tortuous rococo pink German ones, – an assortment of very much overstuffed furniture, and a naked-looking recording machine completed what might well be called the *décor*. A room more tawdry and depressing could not be imagined, and yet when this small man took the fiddle from Patricia and began to play, instantly the room was transformed. . . .

Patricia was learning a Beethoven sonata; she is a pretty girl, healthy and spirited, and she flirted with Izzy. All quite normal, I observed from my corner: to fall in love with one's music teacher accelerates markedly one's progress upon the violin. But after a moment I noticed something queer about this flirtation – it had an edge to it. These two were not sparring like equals; it was the princess and the beggar man, and somebody was not playing fair.

They were launched evenly enough, although the salutation surprised me. None of my fiddle teachers had addressed me thus. "Well, darling," said Izzy, "late again?" – and curled his lip. Patricia pouted; her mouth was admirably suited to the gesture. First there was Ševčik, through which the girl floundered, biting upon the nether cherry. Izzy told her not to mind. "I know you got no time to practise at that fine school where you go." And then there was Beethoven. "My God, my God," said Izzy, and seized the violin. He looked at it, shook his head, and returned it to Patricia. "Work it out for yourself, child," he said. "You got a brain if you want to use it."

Patricia was in no way abashed; she dimpled. She played the phrase, vulgarizing it with an effect impossible to put upon paper. Izzy forgot the cherry lips; he seized his pupil by the shoulder and shook her. "No!" he shouted. "Like this – listen, now – " And he began to sing, *La, la la,* in an astonishingly large and bearish barytone. It was a difficult phrase, with a subtle lead and a subtle ending; I myself had never fully understood it until that moment. I leaned forward from my chair. Now the Lord be praised that had brought me to this room; my fingers itched for Patricia's fiddle.

But Patricia was smiling, laughing outright. She

twisted her lips, moved her head slowly on its long white neck. "I don't think much of your vocal," she told Izzy roguishly.

Izzy shrugged, turning from her for a brief moment; for no accountable reason the blood rose in his pale cheeks. Then he grinned; he put down the violin and began to tell stories; he told them well, with gusto. ". . . And Thibaud said to him, 'Are you the kind of pupil that plays the fiddle at home and practises it in public?' " A pause, then the anecdote about the lady harpist and the singer, then a de Pachmann story: "And de Pachmann played the 'Hammerklavier Sonata,' at the end of a long programme. Forty-five minutes the sonata took, and nobody clapped. He was in a fury. He got up and screamed at the audience. He said, 'De Pachmann played this *sonate* perfectly. But perfectly! You have no applause? It must be that you are ignorant of Beethoven. You do not know the *sonate!* Uneducated beasts, de Pachmann will educate you!' He sat down and played the sonata again from beginning to end, and the audience was so terrified he 'd play it a third time they nearly clapped the house down. . . ."

Another pause. The look oblique, the raised, expectant eyebrow. "Like that one, child?"

Patricia had asked for lessons from this man, at

no inconsiderable price per lesson. She admired the man's art, but she could not throw herself into this admiration. This slight and restless Izzy, with his clothes wrong, his accent wrong – she could not endure that he should have her homage wholly; above all, she could not endure that he should accept it. So she flirted, she turned his art into his person and had her victory. And he knew it. He, in his turn, adored her person, her youth, her beauty, and despised – how bitterly – her blind snobbishness, the limitations of her background, her hereditary point of view. . . .

Patricia glanced at me from the tail of her eye, and put her violin under her chin once more. "Shall I try the Beethoven now?"

"Beethoven?" said Izzy. "You can't play Beethoven, darling. You 're too – young. I 'd never let you touch Beethoven if your mother had n't told me you only want to be an amateur, and she 'd like you to know what it 's all about."

On the way home Patricia was silent a full ten blocks. "Izzy 's too fresh," she said at last. "I don't like the way he calls me 'darling.' "

I replied grimly that I should n't think she would, and at tea before Amanda's fire I put the question direct.

"Pat, what do you think of Izzy?"

"Oh," said the girl, "he 's a marvelous artist, of course." She turned to Amanda. "Heavens, Mother, he knows *everything* about music! When he plays, your jaw just drops. But," she shrugged, "he 's so *queer*. The way he jumps around! His clothes are awful and his accent is funny."

Amanda smiled. "Yes, is n't he ridiculous?"

A voice within me whispered, "Hold back! Softly, now. You 've heard this kind of talk before."

Patricia left the room. "Amanda," I began with beautiful calm and perhaps a little sententiousness, "by what right do you separate the man and the artist?"

Amanda made a sound with her lips. "Oh, don't come here talking social revolution! I 'm glad Pat can discriminate between the right people and the wrong."

Izzy's voice rang in my ears, "Darling, I 'd never let you touch Beethoven if your mother . . ." He had not flaunted the girl openly, had not turned upon her the keen and biting rapier with which he would have pricked to action a real Izzy-pupil. He had told her merely that she was too – young – for Beethoven.

"Izzy," I said to Amanda, "can discriminate, too. All the scorn was n't on Pat's side to-day."

Amanda put down her cup. "Your family is all crazy," she said good-naturedly. "But we don't want Pat to grow up like that. We don't want her to take music too seriously." Real concern came into her voice. "We don't want her to become intense over something, and warped and queer. Such women are unhappy in later life. They don't," she rang the bell for more tea, "they don't make good wives."

I told Amanda she was right. "What you say is unanswerable." I rose to put my cup on the table and it rattled in the saucer. If Amanda was right, then why was I trembling? I dug my hands into my sweater pockets. "No nonsense about you," I said. "Amanda, you are a sensible mother. Your daughter will live a contented, well-balanced life. Her husband will be a fortunate man – " The blood came up in my face; my ears burned. "But don't ask me again, ever, *ever* again, what you asked me yesterday: Why the young generation has no respect for art."

Amanda is, as I have said, an intelligent woman. It is no accident that her children have had the benefits of the best education, the best associations. The musicians who dine at her house are not named Izzy, but Edward; more than once I have played with these Edwards and tried to draw blood from their stone. . . . Standing there, I looked at Amanda and she looked back at me; as the blood beat in my temples, her face seemed to grow proportionately colder, more remote. Silver shone softly in the firelight, rugs glowed deep and rich, from the walls glorious portraits looked down upon us. Books, old and new and well-read, were everywhere. All this was Amanda's; it was the result of years of breeding, of decent living. It was Right, incontrovertible. . . .

Amanda shook her head. We had said little, but when she spoke it was as though we were at the end of a long argument. "That kind of life, that kind of crazy devotion, – living music and playing it and thinking it and *eating* it, – it 's too dangerous," she said.

I went out the door and home. My mother's sister was staying with us; I ran double time up the steps to her door. She was sitting by the window in the old cherry rocker, a book in her hand.

"Why," I asked her, "can't rich people really love art? Why have they no *respect* for it?"

"Because they have n't time," she replied instantly. "Rich people have not nearly so much time as we have. They are always going off on a train or a boat, or someone is calling them up and asking them to be on a committee." She smiled.

"You must n't be so angry. It 's not the lady's fault that she is rich."

I repeated Amanda's conversation, and, as I talked, my aunt leaned forward, her hands tight about the chair arms. "Amanda says it has its place, art, but it 's dangerous when a person becomes too intense about it."

"Too intense?" My aunt can laugh like a whip snapping. "People are n't intense *enough;* that 's the trouble. I 've been painting all my life. In every portrait I 've made, a moment has come when I knew I could n't finish. I 've walked away and put my brushes down and told myself I could n't go on. I could n't get over that hill. A kind of exhaustion – "

"But you walked back. You did finish."

"Yes. That 's the point. But you can't be polite about it. You can't smile. You must keep on, *on!* When it hurts you *here,* in the solar plexus – " she laid a hand on her body; the gray eyes shone hard and bright. "That 's when you must keep on. . . . Rich people, rich women especially, don't understand that kind of fight. That 's why they can't respect the Izzies."

I have two violin pupils, little girls of twelve. One is rich and brilliant, and one is a Quaker and fears God. Between them they long ago upset my preconceived notions about talent and musical progress – or, rather, they caused me to redefine for myself the word "talent." The quick pupil, the brilliant one, is ambitious, determined to learn to play as well as or better than her sister. Yes, and you will learn to play, Joanna, my dear – but will you ever learn *music?* I have watched you, your fiddle under your chin, and I have seen you smile at your mistakes. Funny, is n't it, to hear the notes come wrong? A good joke on Papa Haydn, to make his dotted sixteenths sound like triplets? I have seen you, Joanna, slap your bow against your ankle, I have heard you crack your fiddle against the table leg, – a sound that causes any string player to wince, – and your lovely lashes have not fluttered. Is it that you know too well another fiddle lies waiting in the well-lined nest from which this one was drawn? Easier, oh, easier, for the camel to go through the needle's eye than for you, gifted, unfortunate Joanna, to enter the kingdom of music.

And Patience – straight-haired, silent Patience whose Quaker home has known no music, whose fingers close gratefully around the cheap violin I lend her, and who has had to start miles behind

Joanna's pistol shot? Patience, so shy in the presence of music that weeks passed before I discovered her very keen sense of pitch – Patience has frowned for months over key signatures with which Joanna has been familiar since the cradle. One day I lost my temper with Patience because she was so slow; again and again we repeated the phrase, and again and again she played it wrong. I looked at her violin and upon it lay a watery pool. I thought it was perspiration; I have seen a like pool upon Sascha Jacobson's fiddle after a Schubert quartet – and I asked myself, in the manner of Lady Macbeth, Who would have thought the child had so much lymph in her? Then the child blinked, and blinked again; there was a splash, and I saw from whence flowed this precious pool.

"Patience!" I cried. "How awful of me! How unforgivably awful!"

"I want to get it right," the child said. "It 's a nice piece. *I want to get it right*" – and went on playing.

I do not think that Patience, when she is a woman grown, will ever say, "I adore music, but – "

Once I asked Joe Knoedler how he happened to learn the violin. He replied with a short, revealing biography. "I was born," he said, "on River Street. It's a long way from River Street to the Hill." He looked at me quickly, and looked away. "On River Street there was no money for music lessons. My mother wanted me to play the violin and my father wanted me to play the cello. So I learned both. I learned cello from my uncle and I learned fiddle at the Foundation School. But I didn't dare practise the cello at home because of my mother; she knew it would ruin my hand for the violin. So I used to keep the cello up at my Uncle Levi's and practise there. One day my mother found out. She carried the cello home from my uncle's house to our house and brought it to me and said, 'Joe, which of these fiddles you want to learn? The big one or the little one?' I said, 'The little one,' and what do you think she did? She took the cello and smashed it, right there in front of me. Smashed it and stepped on it. Up till then I'd never seen her throw away so much as a potato peeling. She smashed that cello dead, and then she said to me, 'Now go learn your violin, boy, and learn it right.' "

He paused; when he spoke again his voice was cautious: "She wouldn't have done that on the Hill, would she?"

"On the Hill," I told him quietly, but with that

sensation one sometimes has of yelling with all one's strength, "—on the Hill is not a man or woman that can play the fiddle as you can play it, Joseph Knoedler."

CHAPTER V

A friendly art, and some anecdotal proofs of the saying that all quartet players meet sooner or later

IF it is difficult for the Amandas to cross the bridge halfway to the Izzies, if it is impossible for them to meet upon the bridge's arch and take each other by the hand, it is, by that same token, a swift delight for one musician to recognize another in midstream. When I was a girl of twenty I found myself, one cold morning, whistling to keep my courage up. It was at Skagway, Alaska, at not quite five in the morning, and I was on board the observation train which was to take us over the mountain pass. The cars were open, like a summer trolley; over my right shoulder rose the high, barren hills we were to traverse, while below to my left our steamer lay upon waters flat and colorless in the damp morning air. I was breakfastless and miserable to the bone; I was, indeed, abandoned completely to that state known as "travelers' melancholia." I hated everyone on the ship, including the captain, and everyone on the train, not excluding my good parents, who had brought me there, and the engineer, who could not get the steam up.

So I crouched miserably in the last seat of the last car, and, pushing my hands farther into my coat pockets, wished I were a wolf that I might howl my hatred to the sky. Lacking the equipment for a really good howl, I began to whistle – not to be merry, but because there is a perverse satisfaction, on a cold day, in watching the warm breath of one's bosom ascend coldly in steam. At the moment, I do not believe I could have told you what I was whistling; it was the opening theme from Beethoven's "Spring Sonata," that heavenly tune beforementioned, with a flow, a melodic line that would put the bird to shame. Four measures, I whistled: –

and from up forward somewhere came back, clear and startling, the answering phrase: –

I leaped from my seat and ran forward along the ground. We had been two weeks on the ship and I had met no one who knew a note of music.

There had been an Eskimo on board – named, for some remote Eskimo reason, Harry – who owned a ramshackle violin upon which I had, from sheer homesickness, attempted to play, but Harry, I well knew, would never whistle Beethoven. I remember how the hard ground pounded beneath my feet as I ran, and the genial grin of the whistler when I found him. All the way from Java he had come, a big grizzled Dutchman in gray tweeds, green knee stockings, and a green Bavarian hat with a feather; we sat together and were friends, and the morning air was cold no longer. The engineer got the steam up, my new friend said, "Then you, too, play the 'Fifth Sonata'?" – and off we went, matching measure for measure up the mountain.

Before I met Dr. Lang, the physicist, I used to see him wandering morosely in the lobby of the Academy at symphony concerts, and I thought, "Who is the distinguished cellistic-looking person with the handsome gray hair, and why have n't I the courage to speak to him?" I used to hear him talking, and I liked what he said. One night, standing in the lobby, I heard him inveigh against newspaper reporters. "I stood there in my laboratory and I told those reporters, 'No! Don't print that! *No,* you can't use atomic energy to drive a motor car or to drive anything else.' And they said, 'Professor, did n't you say there was energy in the electron?' I told them, 'Yes. But it 's not convertible for practical purposes, and don't say I said it was, and don't put in your paper that I said you could use atomic energy for anything whatever.' And this morning, there it was in the paper, with my picture: 'Dr. Axel Lang says we will soon harness the electron to drive the motor car, doing away with gasoline entirely.' "

He cast his cigarette gloomily on the floor and dug his heel into it. "Thank God for music," he said, and I turned quickly to my brother John, who was with me, and asked, "Who and what is this man?"

John said, "Don't you know? He plays the cello. Shall I ask him if he 'll come next Sunday for quintets?"

I rejoice that Dr. Lang proved to be more than a physicist; he is a cellist of no mean ability. If the non-musical stomach turns at the phrase, "more than a physicist, a cellist," let me say, rather, I rejoice that this particular physicist leads so large a life. I am glad that he can be counted upon, on a Sunday evening, to bring a viola-playing wife. (Happy the fiddler who boasts a viola wife.) In fact Dr. Lang can be counted upon to bring any number of first-rate professional fiddlers. One Sunday he appeared with enough for an octet, so we played Svendsen – all of us agreeing, afterward, that octets are noisy and we prefer the magic number, four.

One night Dr. Lang told me with a pleased smile that he was going south, to-morrow, to lecture. As I had never seen anything but gloom upon the face of a scientific man about to embark on a lecture tour, I inquired concerning the pleased expression, and he replied quickly that it was to be a combined lecture and concert tour. "In the morning," he said, "I am to lecture on the electron, and then I shall take out my cello and play Handel to the students. At three o'clock I am to talk about matter and energy, at the conclusion of which I shall play the Beethoven 'A Major.' In the evening I address the assembled scientists on the artificial disintegration of the lithium atom, after which – " his face beamed, "I shall give them the Brahms 'E Minor Cello Sonata.' "

I asked him whose idea this was, the lecturer's or the lecturees', and he replied evasively that, Oh, he just happened to mention he played the cello and they said bring it along –

When he returned from the tour, I asked Dr. Lang how it had gone, meaning politely, did he have a satisfactory response from his audience?

His reply could only have been made by a true musician. He never mentioned the audience. He said, "I had a glorious time. I played the Brahms twice over."

Scientists either love music or they hate it; for them there seems to be no middle ground. Einstein is of course the premier example; I have always been glad he is such an excellent violinist; the fact seems, somehow, to ennoble both music and Einstein. I could write a book on Scientist-Fiddlers I Have Known. As ensemble players, scientists are superlatively satisfactory; no other phrase will express it. They are not superlative technicians; they are free, therefore, from all taint of virtuosity; hard workers upon their instruments, they subordinate themselves to the ensemble with the passionate discipline of a patriot soldier. And strangely enough they nearly always have viola wives, or flute wives, or piano wives. The doctors Ostermann, Hand, and Lang all have viola wives; Dr. Houston has not, but he has the next best thing. He has a wife who is headmistress of a large and important school; she comes to quartet evenings, not with a fiddle, but with a thick sheaf of student papers and a blue pencil. All evening she sits contentedly under the lamp making marks with the blue pencil; never once have I heard from her the dreaded wifely remark, "Dear, have n't you played long enough? *Must* you finish that quartet?"

No scientist, no doctor-fiddler, comes to quartets with strings broken from neglect, or a bow arm stiff from lack of practice. Dr. Retinus, second violin in our Tuesday-night quartet, is an ophthalmologist, with an impressive office in the city. I know this office; I took my small boy there to have his eyes examined. There were lady secretaries and outsized telescopes and Turkey carpets and fine etchings – and on the mantel a familiar black fiddle case. "But of course I bring it to town!" cried Dr. Retinus. "I practise every day, after office hours."

And so he does. This man's days, filled with delicate eye operations, with lectures delivered at the university, with scientific papers read in distant cities, with the writing of a large green book about eyes – this man's days include an hour's practice upon the lowly violin. *Fiddling!* From whence the ancient scornful connotation of that word?

"Fiddling?" cried Dr. Retinus, leaping to his feet, standing thus between telescope and violin case – "Fiddling? I could n't live without it."

And he threw out his left arm, the fingers crooked eagerly about an imaginary finger board. He grinned. "Till Tuesday!" he said as I took my leave.

"All quartet players," said Dr. Ostermann, himself an excellent violinist-pathologist, "meet sooner or later." My brother John has a distinct talent, a flair, for picking up cellists. They cannot resist him, nor he them. John, to a cellist, is nothing less than catnip. One night he came home from Washington with the worried expression one seems to have when arguing a case before the Supreme Court. We asked him how the case was going. He could not tell just yet, he replied. "But — " he brightened, "the lawyer that 's opposing me plays the cello. He says he can play Brahms. I 've asked him here for Sunday the eighteenth." John turned to his wife. "Is that all right, Sarah?"

Sarah replied warmly that of course it was all right, but could this man sing, as well as play? "We need," she reminded John, "tenors for the Vaughan Williams 'Benedicite.' "

John, it seems, had not inquired about the lawyer's voice. I asked him a trifle sourly if he was not taking a good deal on faith? And I reminded him that meeting a cellist does not mean meeting a good cellist, and he ought to know that by this time. To which John retorted that if a man did one thing with all his might he was apt to do another the same way, and this Whitelaw was a bang-up good lawyer. "Anyway," John said, "his wife plays viola, so I told him, 'Fine! Bring your wife along on the eighteenth and we 'll have a string quartet if my daughter is at home.' That all right, Sarah?"

Sarah looked surprised. "Why do you keep asking me if it 's all right?" Sarah plays the piano, but what she likes is to sing alto, and she is an excellent sight singer. "All I can say is," she finished, "I hope this Mrs. Somebody is a good high soprano."

The Whitelaws came, on the eighteenth, and stayed not one night but two. The question of their vocal and instrumental capacity belongs to another chapter; I am concerned here only with my brother's talent for enticing stranger cellists. John's enthusiasm is apt, at times, to distress persons not musically inclined. One summer day he boarded the bus for Sandy Bay; it is a tedious journey from Philadelphia to the Jersey coast, and John, who always reads musical scores on the train, was provided with the usual *divertissement*. The bus was crowded and hot; my brother sat down, perforce, next to a large, perspiring fat lady. When the bus was well on its way John drew from his brief case Handel's "Messiah," opened it on his knee, noted the key, – E minor, – took from a pocket his pitch pipe, set it at the dominant, and blew it. He said he blew it quite loudly, because the bus was making a noise, and John's ear is none too sharp. The fat lady was already sunk in a fat doze. "She jumped," related John, disgust in his voice, "as if she had been stuck with a needle." She was terrified. She screamed. She clutched John and said, "Conductor! Conductor! Is there an accident?"

When John told his story, we screamed too, with mirth. But John did not see any humor in it. "Would n't you think," he muttered, "any grown woman would know *B* when she heard it?"

He had better luck with the New York lawyer, not a cellist this time, but a man who, at the very outset of the case, drove John to a frenzy of dislike, and John him. He was the opposing lawyer; they hated each other, John said, from first sight; they could not seem to meet on any ground whatever. One day they were having lunch, wrangling or relapsing into gloomy silence, when John happened to mention Brahms. (And how many breaths can you draw, Brother, *without* mentioning Brahms?) The lawyer brightened, beamed, "raised his head," said John, "and whinnied." He was, it seems, as frantic a Brahmsian as John. He played no instrument, but was actually the possessor, John told us, awe in his voice, of the original manuscript of one of the *Magdelonelieder*. . . . "We went back to court arm in arm," said John, "and from then on the case was smooth and sweet."

Occasionally I meet a man who tells me, "No, I don't know music. I play no instrument and I can't keep a tune" – and yet in my heart I salute him as a potential musician. There is something – an emotional direction, a spiritual predisposition – that is always recognizable. Such persons seek musicians as friends; they will themselves come, sooner or later, to music. Leo is like that. Leo is fifty-five, a practising physician. He neither plays nor sings; he cannot read a note – but where is music, there goes Leo on the run. It has not always been thus, with him. "When I was forty," he told me, "I asked a friend, 'What is this music you talk about and spend money to hear? The people I like best all go to concerts and come out feeling better than when they went in. How can I join this club? What is the password and how may I learn it?' "

His friend told him to go to concerts, "But not just *any* concert. Go this way: Choose some especial piece, say, the 'Fifth Symphony' of Beethoven, and every time you see it on the billboard, go and hear it. And see what happens."

The first time he heard the "Fifth Symphony," Leo was bored. He was bored the second time, and the third. But he is a persistent fellow, and he went again. This time he recognized a tune. "The *andante* tune," he told me. "It was terribly exciting, waiting for the cellos to do that tune. They began to play it, and I knew what was coming next. . . . And the fifth time I heard it, I wanted to cry."

Slowly, patiently, in fifteen years Leo has learned the password to all nine symphonies of Beethoven. "I am going ahead on these lines," he told me, "until I am dead. Ours is a long-lived family. By the time I am ninety I shall be able to walk right up and shake César Franck by the hand. . . ."

But one cannot afford to go barging about, inquiring of the casual stranger, "Do you play music?" Indeed, unless very sure of the answer, there is no question to be put with more caution, no subject to be approached so hesitantly. One does not court disappointment on every street corner, and your true enthusiast – in any line, perhaps – is not to be found in the market place. What was it my aunt had said, "Most people are not intense *enough?*" My very grandest specimens of the species "fiddler" have been found in the most unlikely latitudes. Ernst Hand, for instance. I was living in the woods, one summer, in the middle of Connecticut, and I was not thinking of music at all. There was beauty all about me; there were leaves blowing above the brook, there was tall corn that moved in the south meadow and in the west; at night and in the morning three cows walked by my door with bells around their necks. Also, the cows gave creamy milk, great flowing pitchers of it, and the corn was sweet. All this, and yet a craving filled me. I asked my neighbor, "What is this hunger that gnaws unceasingly at the well-filled belly?" She laughed, and gave me some traveler's directions on a slip of paper. I put on my hat and said to my children, "Children, I am going to Fairweather to play the violin. Do you want to come?"

They inquired if they would have to get washed first, and would there be children there, and some nice dogs for them while I was playing? I said no, and yes, and we leaped in the char-à-bancs and drove to Gilead, Hebron, Willimantic, Putnam, and Windham. Suddenly the sign said, "Fair-weather Town Line." A woman in spectacles was mowing a lawn; I asked her, "Please, does an Ernst Hand live here?" She said, "Dr. Hand from New

York?" I said I did not know about that, but he played the violin. . . .

I found him at the end of the road, the very end. There was an old delicious clapboard house, and a huge barn, upon the roof of which three men were hammering shingles, a pleasant sound. All about were dogs and children. A car had turned in at the gate before me; a young farmer in overalls and hip boots got out. I said, "Oh!" and he said, "*What!*" – and seized me by the hand. It was young Dr. Ostermann, with whom I had but lately played quartets in Concord, over the border. He said, his words coming fast and faster, "I *told* my father I knew that woman in the car back of us. I told him I had played quartets with her somewhere, only you had on those dark glasses. . . . My God, come right in if you're looking for music! All the people in this house play violins."

They did. In that house were a cello, two violins, a clarinet, and an oboe – and a person to go with each. I was ushered into the midst of all these instruments at the particular moment when a large blond child in overalls was having a bloody finger bound by two of the doctors. I said, "Dear me, is your little boy hurt?" – and they replied, "It's a girl and she's learning the cello."

I found myself, my identity still unexplained, being conducted through the woods by my host to see the swimming hole. We saw it, a deep, cool clearness spilling over rocks, shadowed by white birches leaning in a slender, magic circle. We climbed the woody hill again toward the comfortable sound of hammers; my host, still ignorant of my name and the purpose of my visit, said politely, "Did I hear them say you find time during the winter for ensemble playing?"

It was as though he had asked me, Do you find time, then, to eat, time to sleep? So I repeated stupidly, "Time? Time to play my fiddle?"

"In the evenings," he persisted, "you find time then, for quartets?"

"Goodness!" I said. "My heavens, don't *you?"*

He threw back his head and laughed. "That 's it," he said, and we walked on in silence. "Quartet playing," he announced with sudden gravity—"it 's my one great passion."

I asked him which of the family played the oboe I had seen, and he said, Was n't it a beautiful instrument, and he had lately bought it for his wife. No, he replied to my question, Cornelia had never played the oboe, she was the family violinist. "But you see, I play the clarinet. So we both thought," continued this husband confidently, "that Cornelia should learn the oboe."

I agreed. Maritally speaking, it seemed, indeed, an eminently sensible arrangement. I told myself, emerging into sunshine, that Cornelia's name would never be known in the Courts of Domestic Relations and wondered if, in the event of her husband taking up the kettledrum, Cornelia would rise with equal passion to a study of the cymbals?

I know Cornelia better now. I think she would.

A new acquaintance invariably inquires of me, after the exchange of names, whether I do not play the violin? If introduced by my family, the person has received hints already; if we meet on a bus, a passenger boat, a station platform, our encounter is due to the circumstance of the stranger's offering to carry one of my violins. Three violins, two children, and accompanying suitcases place a lady in the position of respectable, but inevitable pick-up. Yes, I reply warily, I play the violin – but I avoid asking, Do you? If they play, they will tell me in the next breath; but if they hesitate, and are very attractive, I hasten to cement the friendship before discovering they are unmusical. This woman, this man, this stranger – what eager, irresistible response-to-life shines from the eye, is revealed in the quick motions of the body! I want to know this person. Let us talk, therefore, of books, of children, of sailing boats — but let me not permit this new-found delightful human to confide that of all songs the "Road to Mandalay" is best, or demand whether I *make* those poor children practise on those violins. Later, when conversation has discovered a mutual passion for New Hampshire hills, John Donne, and September waters under the keel, then let the person declare against symphony as against sin, and our friendship will ride roughshod over the sacrilege.

Sad are the limitations of the fanatic and many the doors that are shut to him — but, Ah, the compensation! It is worth the sacrifice. Comes that man who says, "How do you do? Bad weather for fiddle strings to-day, and do you know the Hallelujah place in 'King David'?"

"Honegger?" I cry, and try it, humming. "No, no," he says. "Like this. It goes like this," and he begins to whistle. I stumble after him, but I cannot catch the rhythm; he pulls a pencil from his pocket and scribbles on the back of a grimy envelope. Together we study the slender marks and together we hum, as he beats time with his right forefinger!

Then we look at each other and smile, and are silent.

So many lovers has the musically-minded! The musically-hearted, I should say. Hastily I deny the implication of music as an aphrodisiac. If lovers, if friends, exchange the quickened glance, the mutual smile at the perfect rendition of a Mozartian phrase, it is not each other they bespeak, but Mozart.

Once – and once only – I met a man on a train with the "G Minor Symphony" of Mozart in his suitcase. Those yellow, paper-backed scores – what lady fiddler could resist them? The gentleman opened his bag, took out the score and a pencil, and sat there, reading. I hummed; I could not help but hum. The stranger turned, took off his spectacles, and said mildly, "You are a third too low." "I am sorry," I replied, adding weakly that it must have been due to the fact that I had always played second violin in that symphony. He then requested me to hum second while he kept the theme, but I stumbled badly over this and had to retreat in confusion. . . .

Music has been called the most abstract, the "purest" of the arts. And yet, of all the arts music is, in a sense, the quickest to reach centre; its very purity, its disinterestedness, its brave quality of belonging to no man, give to it this privilege. A Beethoven sonata has no axe to grind. Like lightning, music strikes through to the heart, having no delay of words, no slow intermediary of language or of those pictorial symbols which travel home through the eye. Impudent futility, to endeavor to translate music into color or poetry or any dimension but its own! As to the indoor occupation of detecting the composer's emotional dates, of counting up his various loves by the purpler passages of his concertos — anyone can attest its foolishness by comparing two or three biographies of one master. John did it, in a book he wrote about Brahms. John says that for Brahms music was far too serious, indeed too sacred a matter to permit any foolish attempt at story-telling. "The clarinet trio does not, as Specht asserts, 'sing but of love alone,' nor is the clarinet quintet, as Miss May and Niemann would have us believe, a 'retrospect' filled with 'resignation' and 'loving regret' that the 'evening is not far away when no man can work.' It is merely the music that Brahms was interested in writing after he had heard Mühlfeld, whom he called a 'stupendous fellow,' play the clarinet, and realized the possibilities of the instrument in combination with strings. These critics forget," says John, "that Brahms was much more interested in music than in any man or woman or event or person, including himself.

Brahms himself told Henschel that in his young days the best songs came into his head while brushing his shoes before dawn."

And it comes sourly into *my* head, Why do not some of these critics, so interpretively exuberant, ascribe the "B Major Trio" to the inspiration of Brahms's best brown shoes? It would make more sense than most of their interpretations and ascriptions.

What happens when the critic attempts to attribute to absolute music a meaning related to external events or even to specific human emotions John demonstrates by paralleling two analyses of the last part of the Brahms "F Minor Piano Quintet":—

Niemann	*Specht*
	The sinister wrestling and sombre piano quintet . . . mighty and wrathful . . . whose darkness is lightened only by the melancholy and yet steadfast *andante*. . . . Born of defiant melancholy, it belongs to the gloomiest and greatest music Brahms has ever written.
The finale . . . in spite of the minor key . . . is thor-	The introduction to the finale . . . leads to a rondo

oughly contented and jovial, inclined to all sorts of amusing little rhythmical tricks, and altogether sportively disposed.

which takes its ease and yet seems to find no comfort. Restless semiquavers in thirds, succeeded by quavers, pulsate through it; the whole is relentlessly whipped onward by syncopation; the curiously songless, exclamatory second subject, with its jerking upbeat, brings no ray of light into the movement.

The coda . . . goes laughing by till it is finally concentrated still more drastically by means of syncopations. Yet all this does not succeed in checking its joyful moods; and, in the concluding lines, it takes its leave by breaking off abruptly as though with bright ringing laughter.

The end of the piano quintet is as spacious and serene as its opening is grave and full of pathos.

The expansive coda where the themes, dissolved into a more and more precipitate triplet motion, chase each other in the manner of a *stretto,* dashes toward the dark unknown. The composer's heart must have been desolate indeed when he wrote this study in black.

Painfully born of the composer's soul . . . with its atmosphere of exalted joylessness.

Strange, that men will not let music be music, but must transform it into bright ringing laughter, studies in black, or dashes toward the dark unknown!

Against all this overdone romanticism and against romanticism's consequent, an overdone realism, the modern musician leans to the extreme of ascetic reaction, and attempts to dehumanize music altogether. A surfeit of programme music, a surfeit of orchestral factory whistles and machine-gun fire, and we have drawn in the emotional belt until we are thin to the point of emaciation. In our city the symphony conductor desires his orchestra in a sunken pit, out of sight, and he is raising money to put it there. He says the sight of the players distracts the audience; he says – but anyone can imagine what he says. Well, and what I say is, he is too much the purist, and he will lose a subscriber. Romantic interpretations of a symphony are misleading and silly, but in the honest mechanism of an orchestra is nothing of either quality. Were this tempest of sound produced by electric wires and a push button, I should desire wires and push button out of sight – but it is *men* who make this music. I want to see those fiddlers; I want to watch the bow arms moving up and down, and I want to watch the kettledrummer, himself as round and deep and sure as the sound he commands with such triumphant blows of the stick. . . . The cymbal player – what would Tchaikowsky's "Pathétique" be without those wide-flung arms in the *allegretto?* I want to see the harpist tune her lovely instrument, leaning her brown head against the strings, and I want to see, above his magic flute, Kincaid's raised eyebrows and expressively movable scalp. . . .

Sink them in a pit, Maestro? Sink yourself in a pit! Must we then feel shame that we enjoy the sight of our own flesh and blood? A too vigorous asceticism, this separation of body and spirit, of musician and music. A fiddle is not a fiddle until it touches a human shoulder, until it is tucked warmly under a human chin. One day a man argued with me, thus: "Woman, you say the word 'Beethoven,' and you draw in your breath. Come now, if the 'Fifth Symphony' bore no signature, if it had been written compositely by fifty million people, would n't it still be as great?"

"No," I replied, "and again, no!" And I thought wearily that this question, so often repeated, was as irritatingly beside the point as the bird remark: "That robin can beat Brahms hollow." Why does man so persistently endeavor to detract from the glory that is man? What fear, what false shame, causes him to deny his own divinity? The "Fifth Symphony," what is it but the expression of fifty million people, filtered through the man that was Beethoven? Fifty million men struck deaf in the midst of such fullness of sound as only the gods enjoy, fifty million men fighting each his fate with the defiant courage of despair, fifty million voices crying out, at the end, in gratitude to their Maker. *"Heiliger Dankgesang,"* wrote Beethoven above one of his last great string quartets – *"Heiliger Dankgesang eines Genesenen an die Gottheit."* Nor was he thanking his God for recovery from mere bodily illness; here was recognition to God for the final gift of reconciliation, for that serenity which, as Wagner said in speaking of its expression in these later quartets, passes beyond beauty.

Music is aloof, and music is friendly – intimate to the heart as the heart's own beat. There are persons who can prove that Shakespeare never existed, that Jesus never existed, and that Beethoven's symphonies would have been as great if written compositely. But surely the Idea, however godly, however spiritual, needs a vessel, needs to pass, for its birth and interpretation, through that most warm and bloody filtration found only in the frail, absurdly vulnerable arteries of man.

CHAPTER VI

Music and marriage, with especial mention of viola wives and of their antithesis, the lady unduly artistic

THE viola is an excellent instrument for wives. It is not a solo instrument, it is the alto voice — an excellent thing in women. Placed midway between solid bass and brilliant soprano fiddle, the viola is your perfect instrument of ensemble, its spirit that of sturdy, self-respecting subordination.

I have known three very satisfactory violists who were also extremely satisfactory as wives. You may, if it suits better your sense of values, turn the sentence round the other way; for myself, not being a husband, I prefer the statement as it stands. The viola is not, on the face of it, a woman's instrument. It is large and bulky; to produce a real viola tone requires strong fingers; to sustain such a tone, no inconsiderable muscular endurance. The three wives I speak of are all amateurs; two of them are married to professional musicians. The first of these was encountered in student days in

Baltimore; the charming household Van Bart gave me that revelation of delight which was my first string quartet, my first glimpse, indeed, of real *Haus-musik.*

Van Bart directed the quartet; we played in his room in the Conservatory, a bare, bright room with skylight and ancient, dusty grand piano – a room that came alive when the four of us were seated at the stands and Van Bart had struck the air with his right forefinger. I, whose acquaintance with wine had been limited to a taste of my father's claret at dinner, a gulp of whiskey in the bathroom tumbler when I was catching cold, breathed wine in that dusty room. And I breathed a headier wine when Van Bart, selecting three of us from the string pupils, invited us to his house in the country. Every Sunday we played there, Mrs. Van Bart at – as the phrase goes – the viola. Perhaps the phrase does not properly go that way unless applied to the piano or the bat, but it fits Mrs. Van Bart. She went, indeed, *at* the viola. She tore it to pieces; not before or since have I heard a viola emit such crucifying sounds. Mrs. Van Bart suffered from these sounds as much as any of us, for she was truly musical, but she never apologized. She made faces, she drew in her breath through her teeth, but she never apologized.

Our cellist was excellent; I have forgotten her name, but I recall with pleasure her smooth dark hair and bright cheek at the cello's neck, the round resonance of her tone. My place as first fiddle was easy because Van Bart always stood by and conducted. Once when he had a cold he conducted from his bed in the next room; when he called me in to unravel some repeated stupidity, I was paralyzed with shyness. This was, I believe, the first time my careful Philadelphia existence had ever included a man in bed. But I knew instantly that no male of my clan could wear successfully those wild, delightful striped silk pajamas, that no room in our house could achieve at the same time so crazy a disorder and so indubitable, so exhilarating a style. I stood in the doorway, violin in hand, and a voice from the bed, stopped with cold, a little irritated, said to me: –

"Come in, Miss Dr-rinkair! Why do you stand there dumb like a fish? Do not take the sixteenth notes so fast and do not, for the love of God, slur the last one in the measure. How many timces –" he pronounced the word with a *c* in it – "how many timces must I remind you? Such an effect! Vulgar – A-ah! Give me your fiddle – here – play the notes evenly, all alike. Not to hurry, not to be gasping for breath like a hookèd trout. . . . So!"

It mattered not if I were called fish twice in the same breath; halibut or God-forsaken amateur – let them name me what names they chose, if only they would let my fiddle in their door. As to the Van Barts, well or sick, they were always jolly. Van Bart's interest in our very uncertain playing never flagged; when his wife committed some too flagrant atrocity, he would whack her on the shoulder and she would give vent to some loud foreign ejaculation and recover herself. . . . The old stone house was furnished in oak and pewter, things Mrs. Van Bart had brought from Holland; the three round-cheeked Van Bart sons tumbled and shrieked about the room, but nobody rebuked them. The place was full of animals, shaggy dogs, cats, birds in cages – and I loved it. At some indeterminate time during the evening we would have supper before the fire – cold meat, bread, cheese, and beer. When the Van Barts began to eat and drink they became even jollier. They roared with laughter, they pounded on the table, they fed the dogs with huge chunks of meat. Van Bart at such times lost his dapperness, his man-of-the-world veneer; he would seize Marya, the dark-eyed little second violinist, and kiss her heartily. I know that I became very silent, a little awed. Not so was Sunday evening conducted in Philadelphia. The Van Bart boys were never put to bed; they fell asleep anywhere, on the floor, on the wooden settles before the fire. . . . Van Bart would tease me. "She sits there, so white and still with her face of a Madonna. To whom do you pray, Madonna? What god watches over musicians in your Philadelphia? What pa*tron*?"

It was to John I prayed. In my life, until then, music had had but one patron, although it was to have many before it came, at the last, to have no patron but itself. I think all virgins have magic phrases that their hearts repeat; I knew of one girl who used to chant, at those moments when mentality is suspended, *"I'll find it. I'll find it soon."* . . . And my chant, when hard-pressed between musical enthusiasm and a fiendish shyness that paralyzed my fingers and rendered my bow arm weak and wispy – my chant concerned the name of John. "John," I would whisper, "help me! I can't get the rhythm." Or, "John! I've got it. Hear me, John; this is music!" And sometimes, when the name of music had been taken in vain, when I found myself in drawing-rooms at tea time, on school platforms at Commencement, – caught in a false situation, playing the "Méditation" from *Thaïs,* the "Barcarolle" from the *Tales of Hoff-*

mann, showing off with outworn tools for ladies with gloves upon their hands, – then I would apologize furiously: "John! I don't mean it. I know it is n't music." . . .

Such was the household Van Bart, and the first viola wife my life encountered. The other two viola wives, while as effective in their way as Mrs. Van Bart, are effective more by design than by instinct or that easy, contagious appetite for music that ruled the establishment Van Bart. . . . Mrs. Whitelaw, married to that indefatigable lawyer-cellist whom we have met before, was invited by John "on spec," as it were, to come to Philadelphia with her husband and play. The day of their arrival was Sunday, and it rained. It began early, a cold November mist that drove against the long windows of the music room. At breakfast John looked at the weather with glee in his eye. "Ha!" he said. "We can play all day. We won't have to go for a walk and we won't have to ask anybody if they 'd like a little golf – "

We did play all day; with time out for dinner and tea and supper, we were at it for eight hours. The Whitelaws performed well, excellently well. I know nothing of Mr. Whitelaw in the law courts save what John has told me, but for all those hours

I sat across the music stand from him and saw no sign of weakening other than a slight, repeated sniffle toward the eighth hour. John was right; an adult who is indefatigable at one exercise is likely to be indefatigable at another. The following month I went to New York and spent a night with the Whitelaws to play quartets; Mrs. Whitelaw – a powerful woman – confessed that her shoulder had been lame for a week after her visit to us. "But I did n't want to stop playing," she added hastily.

String quartetists never do want to stop playing. Once I played quartets with Max Jacobs at his farmhouse in Bucks County, Pennsylvania. Max is a professional violinist who makes a living coaching amateur ensemble groups; like the busman on holiday, he had invited us and our fiddles to the farm. It was midsummer, very hot and still; we played upstairs by candlelight. Long windows opened upon dusty fields; in our intervals of playing, crickets chanted a dusty chorus. Max's pupils sat on the floor listening – those who could stay awake; in the summers Max's barn is a dormitory for fiddling children. Sascha went to sleep on the hearth that night; so did Ben. But Rachel stayed awake, leaning her dark head against my chair; at one in the morning, Max put down his violin and turned to her. "Child," he said solemnly, "Rachel — never marry an amateur violinist! He will want to play quartets all night."

Of all the long-distance players I have known, Dr. Richard Cabot of Boston is champion. He is insatiable. Like Joe Knoedler, Dr. Cabot does not say, "I am having a good time." Simply, it does not occur to him to stop. And like John, like every academically sincere music player, Dr. Cabot takes all the repeats. He believes in repeats; not only does he take them in minuet and trio, but in the slowest *largo,* in the most interminably numerous variations. When one plays with Dr. Cabot there is never the customary shouted query at the end of the first *allegro,* — the middle repeat has of course been accepted, — *"Repeat?"* The three of us plunge on and take it, without question. . . . A lawyer-violinist with whom I play in Buffalo — like the sailor and his girl, we fiddlers have a quartet in every port — told me he played with Dr. Cabot one night last summer. After the other three players were completely exhausted, Dr. Cabot sighed, shook his head, and remarked, "I have been playing quartets for forty years, and never yet have I found people who would play as long as I wanted."

I wish I had the endurance of some viola wives

I have known. Often, toward the finale of the third quartet, I am conscious of being, as my forefathers would have had it, only a woman. Fatigue creeps upon me; I feel it coming – first my knees, then the middle of my back, then my elbows. Dr. Retinus, who is another Dr. Cabot for endurance, sits at my left with his fiddle on Tuesday nights; he seems to sense what is happening to my elbows and my shoulder blades, but he never says, "Want to stop a minute?" It is Joe Knoedler who pronounces these blessed words, and for the reason that his own enormous back – fortunately for me – collapses at intervals. What Dr. Retinus says is very different. He looks at me gloomily, shakes his head, and remarks, "That 's what it is to have a *woman* in the quartet." I remember well one evening when we played the Brahms "A Minor Quartet." Joe Knoedler loves Brahms; he sailed into this one with his hair on end, his shoulders swinging. When the last chord had sounded, he sprang to his feet; his face was scarlet, his eyes popping. "A man," he said, "could get apoplexy, playing that piece."

"But not," I thought, "a woman." I did not feel apoplectic, I felt limp. All the blood in me had gone somewhere else – down to my toes, maybe. I staggered to the sofa and, laying my head upon

Henry's greasy cello bag, felt warmth flow back to my cold forehead. . . .

But Mrs. Whitelaw is made of no such watery stuff. I wonder if it was for her quality of endurance that Mr. Whitelaw, in the beginning, courted her? When he was a young man he met this girl, one night, playing piano quintets. She was the pianist, and he married her. Before very long she made the discovery that all wise pianists make sooner or later – string players much prefer string ensemble to piano ensemble. The piano is a glorious instrument, but not so glorious, for steady diet, as that other instrument, composed of two fiddles, a viola, and a cello – a string quartet. Marvelous works have been written for piano and strings; what more inspiring than the Brahms "Piano Quintet," what more romantic than the Schumann "E Flat Major Piano Quartet"? I would as soon forfeit a year of my life as my knowledge of these compositions.

But your ensemble player is a creature of habit; he plays, if he is a real enthusiast, regularly, say once a week. Sunday nights, Tuesday nights. And after the three hundred and sixty-fifth Tuesday night, something begins to happen which I have learned to dread. The piano – let me say it in all humility – begins to clatter. What, thinks the first violinist, is this loud noise to my left? To my right, all is harmony, the perfect blending of four instruments of a kind – four brown backs and four brown bellies cut from the tree, strung to hand-turned pegs, varnished with what magic we know not, and mellowed with age. Naturally, they speak with one voice. But this other creature, metal-ribbed, ivory-throated, is he not a bit too insistent with his pedals, too bold with his loud *arpeggio?* Quietly, colleague, quietly – I cannot hear the melody. The second fiddle has the melody and it is obscured by your skillful accompanying triplets. . . . Only a pianist of highest skill can make his instrument blend with strings. And yet no harpsichord could solve this problem; the harpsichord is overlight, underweight, to act as balance to four healthy fiddles.

String players seldom admit in words this piano antagonism – the defense is too apt to be, if not convincing, at least overwhelming. What happens is that the quartet, eventually, meets alone; the pianist is not invited. Said Mrs. Whitelaw to me, – wise Mrs. Whitelaw, who, as a virgin, played only the piano, – "I heard my husband sigh with relief when there was no piano. I heard him tell the other three fiddlers, 'Now, fellows, we can really listen to each other' — and I set to work immediately and learned viola."

So well did she learn it that her husband, far from including her in the music for politeness' sake, seeks constantly her support. He is still the more skillful player of the two, but she is the more decided, shall I say the more insistent, character. Anyway she knows rhythm and she knows music, and when Mr. Whitelaw gets lost, when he begins to sink, he looks at her with the left eyebrow raised and she reaches out, as it were, and, grasping him firmly by the collar, draws him to safety. Sometimes she does not wait for the raised eyebrow; she says, *"Horace!"* and taps with her foot, and Horace, nodding with the benign cheerfulness that is his nature, scrambles hastily back to shore.

That is Mrs. Whitelaw. . . . The third viola wife is perhaps more wife than violist, but then — she has a testy husband. Not unattractively testy, — he is a professional musician, — but a husband that requires delicate handling, and delicate handling takes time and energy. Mrs. Sereno's viola playing, done, perhaps, with what is left over, is a little feeble, but she is there on time, musically speaking; she never loses the place, nor does she tire and want to stop. She is as round and soft as her husband is lean and hungry, and her viola's voice is like her own, hushed and pleasant and a bit deprecatory. She is always ready to play what the rest of us want to play. "Yes, yes," she will assent eagerly, "let us, by all means, begin with Mozart. You are right, it is good to begin the evening with Mozart and, as you say, work up to Brahms." In a family where the five playing members are wont to shout, all at once, the names of their five favorite composers, this soft assenting voice comes as nothing short of a miracle. The lady has become a byword with us. "Why can't you say yes, like Mrs. Sereno?"

But I am not sure, in my heart, about saying yes. By saying yes, Mrs. Sereno achieved security, peace, and Mr. Sereno – but is Mr. Sereno worth all those yeses? Is anybody? Amanda would tell me I have my values confused; what matters is not Mr. Sereno's value to his wife, but vice versa. As wife, Mrs. Sereno has neither time nor spirit to put into a fiddle – into the fierce and hungry maw of music. And this is as it should be. In the Eternal Ledgers, Amanda would say, a wife outbalances a violist fifty to one. . . .

But Mrs. Van Bart did not say yes – not, that is, in the Sereno manner. Mrs. Van Bart had her cake and ate it. I do not know her secret, but I can make a humble guess. Mrs. Van Bart, with her husband, her sturdy sons, her shaggy dogs, her house buried deep in laughter, music, and completest disorder – Mrs. Van Bart had mastered the art of neglect. The question asked me in the Connecticut woods, – Have you time for music? – although it needed, that day, no reply, has an answer and Mrs. Van Bart had found it. It was she who gave me my first hint, my first glimpse of what neglect, properly handled, can mean to a wife and mother.

When people say, "How have you time for so much music, besides writing, tending children, keeping house, and traveling by the cars?" we have now, as a family, a reply. "It is managed," we say, "by a shrewd system of neglect."

Neglect is truly an art. I began exercising it at music school, and my progress was, at first, slow. Learning to practise the violin in a room with an unmade bed was the first test I put myself. I lived in a rented room; the maid did not come to brush it up until late in the morning; if, returning from my cafeteria breakfast, I yielded to the temptation to make the bed, it led inevitably to larger sins, such as dusting or straightening bureau drawers, and a precious hour was fled, wasted and unappreciated. At first, I used to turn my back to the bed, – Satan behind one is always less potent, – but as I improved in virtue and in grace I found I need not close my eyes to these rumpled blankets, that barren mattress; I could sit right in front of them, staring at them, and play scales, bow exercises, the most mechanical and dullest fiddling chores, and not be lured into so much as a pull at the undersheet.

This was the first step. Other victories followed, such as not darning one's stockings until the holes got above the shoe, and then doing them upon the foot. Four years of this stringent discipline prepared me beautifully for marriage – a sudden marriage into a snug home which boasted not only a maidless kitchen, but, very soon, a nurseless nursery.

In this latter estate, where would I and my fiddle have been without the rigors of that long, self-imposed training in the subtle art of neglect? I will admit to moments of failure, moments – nay, months and years – when we slipped too easily into sin, when we let our G string rust, our sound post come unglued, while we taught regular habits to babies, or bleached white rompers upon the line. In fact, the time came when we knew we should have to stop a minute and think – or lose music altogether. What should we do. mv fiddle and I?

Abandon music, abandon household – or make a compromise?

That I compromised is due wholly to that early training. Because of it I knew, not *what* to neglect, perhaps, but *how* to neglect it without twangs of the conscience followed by tedious apologies to husband. Show me a husband that wants to know *why* the living room was not dusted to-day. . . .

Gradually I made music a part of the daily routine. I put my daughter into blue jean overalls and cut her hair to a crop that proved quicker to the brush than prideful yellow shoulder curls. Some inherited remnant of common sense caused me *not* to demand a studio, nor did I declare for the one living room in the house for two hours daily of uninterrupted practice on the violin.

As well for a young wife to demand the Kohinoor diamond. I practised, – it smacks horridly of the Mother's Column, – I practised while my sponge cake was baking – forty minutes – or while Baby Number 2 took his nap, Baby Number 1 being jailed securely in her pen outside the window. In spite of rumors to the contrary, children of three or four will coöperate in this kind of thing. Perhaps the word is resignation rather than coöperation; also I will admit to occasional lapses into the discredited, old-fashioned system of reward and bribery. To what higher use could peppermint or cookies be put? . . . In the evenings I used often to practise in the kitchen; this was in the beginning, when I had my first hazy glimpses of that thing called compromise and felt vaguely that it might be useful domestically, as it had been at school. Also, I had not yet learned that a violin disturbs a sleeping child no more than the windy trees that brush the nursery roof.

It was in my kitchen that I memorized the entire Bach "E Major Concerto" – a difficult feat for one whose only musical facility is in sight reading. I memorized it from sheer bravado, to see if I could, now I was a mother. For months, my neighbors had warned me with sly shakes of the head, "You won't find yourself so ready to play that violin when you have a baby to look after." Indeed, while still a girl at music school, I had listened to dreary prophecies concerning the inappropriateness of musical training where marriage was concerned, my passionate defenses falling shattered against the final argument: "But what would you do with a *baby?*" How could I tell what I would do? Even Papa Goetschius, the renowned counterpoint master, had confronted me in class before grinning rows of dark-haired students. "So you are to be married, young lady? And what about counterpoint?" I remember his malignant black eye. "You will come back to us. Counterpoint is more interesting than cradle rocking."

I am not at all sure of Papa Goetschius's premise, philosophically speaking. Nor do I think the two should be compared – babies and counterpoint! Even there at school, the very fact that I wanted babies and knew I wanted them caused me to work more feverishly at my violin. "If I can get hold of it," I thought, "if I can really get hold of music, I shall be able to keep it always. Twins or triplets or taking in washing will not be able to tear music from me. . . ."

So I cradled my baby and played Bach to the pots and pans upon the wall, hurling triumphant challenge at the false prophets. I forgot every note of that concerto the week after I had learned it; I shall never have enthusiasm or initiative to memorize it again. But neither shall I ever hear those hearty opening sixteenths without an instantaneous vision: five cook pots upon a yellow wall, two big ones, two little ones, and a black-handled frying pan.

Nothing is more to be deplored than the unduly artistic wife: that lady who insists, not only upon a studio all trimmed in batik, but upon devoting three hours before high noon to her Art – and the devil take the household. This eternal question of how much right a wife has to be herself. . . . I cannot help thinking the answer lies, not in how much the wife can be herself, but in that degree to which she can forget herself. Is it Beethoven she pursues upon her piano; is it *music,* or is it her own self-aggrandizement, the chance to show her facile fingers in a *scherzo prestoso?* Perhaps it is this latter trait which, though they may not know its name, so infuriates husbands. Many a wife have I heard sigh, "I gave up my music" (*my* music, she calls it!) "long ago. George just could n't stand it."

And neither could I, George. Because if it were music your wife wanted, if it were a closer acquaintance with Beethoven that she craved, she could get it decently, solo or quartet, while you were at the office. Also, in all likelihood there would be no complaint in her, but only a large crusade; she would teach Beethoven to you and to your children and your children's children. . . . I know a wife who always practises her violin in the kitchen – but for a very different reason than I did. She has no babies to disturb, has Belinda, but she has a George. She told me, at first, that she practised in the kitchen so as not to disturb George in his study. Lest this be misinterpreted as crankiness on the husband's part, Belinda later protested that the bare-walled kitchen was more resonant than the other rooms. "Like singing in the bathtub," I suggested, and Belinda, glancing at me a trifle suspiciously, agreed. Then she laughed, and confided in me the real reason. George, it seems, is a very domestic man and enjoys a domestic atmosphere; he likes to pass through the kitchen while his wife is making jelly; from his study after supper he is comforted by the far-off tinkle of Belinda's dishes in the pan. George admitted, said Belinda, that in the beginning he had feared a fiddling wife might prove too gypsy for him, and that, in some obscure way he could not himself define, it had worried him a little when she played alone in the darkened music room at night. "Why don't you play in here?" he asked her one evening, walking through her bright kitchen on his way to put the furnace to bed, and without argument – as becomes the wise wife – Belinda had complied.

But the adjustment is not always so easy. I know of one sincerely musical wife, at least, whose marriage ended in the divorce courts. Her George was an intelligent man, tolerant of all things save one – music. Himself unable to keep a tune, he hated music with a passionate intensity. He called it the lowest of the arts, all emotion, no intellect – a debauch. Music was whiskey, a drug, a dangerous excitant, a dissipation. "Look," he said, "what it does to the people who live by it, the professional musicians! What are they but unstable egotists, greedy exhibitionists?" It was impossible for this man to believe that anybody really loved music. His wife went to concerts because it was the thing to do; she went to the neighbor's to play piano duets because the neighbor's husband was her lover. Nothing could convince this George to the contrary – and indeed I do not know what argument could convince a deaf man of sound, a blind man of sight, if he considered sound or sight immoral as well as inconvenient.

The spirit in which a household receives music is to me a matter of enormous interest. On winter afternoons I sometimes play piano and violin sonatas with the neighbors; those pianists who happen to be parents show a natural eagerness to see their young seduced to music, and it pains me to observe the contrary methods by which the seduction is often attempted. As we play, children come in, stamping snow from their boots, dragging hockey sticks; over my shoulder I see them in the music-room door, whispering together, watching us. Now is the time, now is the essential precious moment, for parent at piano to cry, "Hi, Georgie! Come in! You and Bill can roast apples at the fire if you will promise not to talk." Many an apple roasted close to the moving bow arm has won its consumer to Beethoven.

On the other hand, how fatal and how frequent that other move, that command: "Katinka! Hush! Come right here this instant and sit on that chair until we are done playing."

Most mothers, whether or no they love music themselves, urge it upon their progeny. I have observed that in those rare instances where the male parent shows an interest, the battle is won before it begins. In a household where father is pianist, a little girl plays the violin. She and I take turns, a movement each; while I do my turn Carolina sits very close, a live kitten on each arm. It annoys her a little that I will not cherish the kittens while she plays; she looks upon me with reproach when I tell her kittens make me sneeze.

It went differently in that far city where I took my violin for a month one winter. There I played in a house where the chatelaine indubitably loved both music and her six children. A beautiful house, large and gracious, with wood fires burning and maids to stop the telephone from ringing. The lady was handsome and spirited; my fiddle was barely drawn from the case when she told me she practised *hours* every day – and flung herself upon the piano. Instantly, as music sounded through the house, a small boy appeared at the door; he walked to me and stood by my shoulder; when we were done playing he put up a hand to touch my fiddle. With a look of ineffable satisfaction he placed it beneath his chin.

"Jimmy," his mother murmured, "is taking piano lessons, but we have a good deal of trouble, don't we, darling?" She turned restlessly to the keyboard. "Run up to the nursery now, dear, and don't make a noise over our heads. Mother wants this hour undisturbed."

The first time I went to this house my hostess told me, "I have taken up silhouette cutting. I am *thrilled* with it. I wanted something to do with my hands." The next Tuesday she said, "Look! I have bought these two fat books in Italian. I shall surely get through them this week." On the final Tuesday she almost ran to meet me. "I have taken up Yogi!" she cried. "See! This is what we do – " And she sank cross-legged to the floor and gazed raptly toward her middle. . . . Crossing the room with my fiddle case, I saw lying open on the sofa a huge paper-backed volume – nothing less than a *Grundriss der Geschichte,* and the lady's handkerchief marked her page. . . .

How could anyone possess such a lust for doing?

Was it in the glands? Was it in the red corpuscles? In the original gene? I tuned my fiddle and sat down, feeling a little depressed. We played for two hours, without pause except when tall glasses of soda water were brought to us. "Energizing," my hostess said. "I always take it" – and tossed it down. I asked myself why I did not get up and go, but something held me inexorably to the score: if she could do it, I could do it. . . . On and on we dragged; my violin sulked, hung back; it was soundless, it peeped like a chicken; the piano roared round me. My fiddle and I were enveloped, drowned in piano. I wondered how long I had been repeating, under my breath, with the violence of exhaustion, "Damn the piano. Damn the piano." At four-fifty – in this kind of bout, one's eye remains glued to the clock – it was suggested that we finish one short movement. Suppressing the urge to declare that the movement I desired was extremely short, and toward the door, I complied, after which Mrs. Blank stood up briskly. She had promised, she said, to go to a tea for the Artists' Relief. I heard my voice remarking that she could perform no timelier act, and I looked up sharply, but she had not heard me.

I went straight to the train; all night the wheels

beneath me pounded in horridly reminiscent six-eight time. In the afternoon we sighted home shores, but I had perforce to go direct from the station to Professor Von Gieringen's, where I was to play sonatas with the professor at the harpsichord. I had never played with harpsichord and had looked forward to it to-day, but I arrived with eye so tired it scarcely noticed the beauty of this small slim instrument, its maple back grained and glowing. A modern harpsichord with two manuals, made in Germany to the professor's order. Heavily I lifted fiddle to shoulder; the professor changed one pair of glasses for another and laid his hands upon the keys. "One moment," he said, fumbling with his feet upon the pedals. I drew my bow slowly down the strings – a long, light bow for a Handel *andante*. . . .

And my violin sang. Soared! All alone by itself, it took wing and left me. I could not believe it – this lovely, woody, *violin* sound. Fatigue vanished; I could hear everything, all my fiddle had to say. No forcing of the tone, no pressure; my fingers scarcely touched the bow. I heard not only the song, the tune, but I heard that other sound beloved of fiddlers – the hiss of rosin against a hard tight string. I was conscious of a hum, a ring, an under-buzzing. I have no word for the rough, sweet magic of the authentic *string* sound. This, at last, was a violin!

The movement was ended. "Do you like it?" the professor asked.

Like it? . . . I demanded quickly why my fiddle had sounded like that. Because he was a musician, because the harpsichord was softer than the piano?

The professor smiled, and gave all credit to his instrument. The harpsichord, he reminded me, is not a percussion instrument. It plucks; it has a string sound, not a hammer sound. "Your violin," he said, "has nothing to fight. Instead of a battle, you have support."

Instead of a battle, you have support. That, I knew suddenly, should be a definition for marriage as well as for music. "I am glad," I told the professor heartily, "that you are a father and a husband. Your household is fortunate." He looked at me oddly and inquired if I would like some nourishment before we played again. Some beer? Some tea, very strong? Some cognac? Was I, perhaps, tired? He went into his kitchen and I did not trouble to tell him that neither nourishment nor stimulus could settle the question that agitated my mind. A question larger, I knew now, than marriage or the law; what barred music from certain households was that thing which barred all harmony from those same thresholds. Not deaf ears or stupid brains, but that old enemy, the ancient tempter. Call him Satan, call him Ego. Insatiable serpent that lies coiled in every breast, ready to strike and destroy all music, all harmony, all things of balance and abiding joy. . . .

If we could have, not music to express already overarticulate personalities, not art for the artist, but the artist for art! If we could have that, Amanda would not be searching out marks, black or white, in the Eternal Ledger, and Mrs. Sereno would have less need to say yes. . . .

Looking back, I see I have written a chapter on compromise, on how to be a musician though married, on the joys of wifely self-sacrifice—and it makes me faintly uneasy. How smoothly, with what sugar of virtue, it dripped from the pen, with its talk of pots and pans and bassinets! Amanda might have written it herself. . . .

Amanda? Mrs. Sereno? Their battle is done and they are the victors. As for me, let me show my true colors. Peace? It is the greatest luxury on earth. Wives? Husbands? I would hang fifty wives, sixty husbands on a tree as against two lines of Beethoven Opus 132. Mothers of children, said Katherine Mansfield, grow on every bush.

No one ever said that about good fiddle players.

CHAPTER VII

God makes the viola players, but ego makes the soloists. Including the suggestion that perfect pitch is a perfect nuisance

It would be timely, after the highly colored peroration of the last page, to abandon the problem of Music and Marriage and the Great I Am, but I cannot do this because there remains a subject, of traditional importance in marriage, upon which I have scarcely touched. I refer to husbands. I have written of fathers and of tone-deaf, unsympathetic husbands. But meek husbands? Musical husbands? Much remains to be said in their favor and disfavor.

It puzzles me to observe that persons who love each other, who have had ample time to make loving each other an easy, daily habit, can exist side by side, day after day, in total ignorance of what the partner is thinking. I had been given to understand that love sharpens the perceptions. . . .

The other night I went out to dinner. Twenty people at a long, glittering table and nineteen of them whole-heartedly horsey, awesomely expert in the hunting of foxes. I admired these people. They were lean and direct, or thick, ruddy, and direct, with clear hard eyes. And they wore their clothes with style. After dinner, while the men sat at table, a woman began to talk to me. I had not seen her before that night, but at dinner someone had told me of her poems. "I never have time to write," she said gloomily. "Horses, horses, always horses. Up at four every day, hacking off to some meet. And all summer schooling colts–"

I wondered why anyone with colts to school and a perfect dress perfectly trimmed with ermine tails should want to write verses *anyway,* and I inquired if she did n't like horses?

She loved horses, the lady said. Heavens, yes. But George was so funny about it. He would n't let her miss one hunt, not one single run. He was positively queer about it. He seemed to take it personally. She did n't dare, she said, miss a hunt to write a poem. She had a novel in mind, but with George feeling this way she did n't see, really, how she was to get a book started.

The husbands came in from the dining room; a handsome man of perhaps fifty, thick-ruddy-direct, introduced himself and sat down. Without preamble, with no word on my part whatever, he commenced telling me what a splendid thing it was for married women to have careers. "Now, my wife writes poetry. She gets it published. She has a novel in mind, too. I tell her, 'Fine, Georgina. Get on with it!' That 's the kind of spirit, that 's the kind of ambition I admire in a woman." He lit a cigarette and flung the match into the fire – *zip!* – as if he were throwing it at a target. "My wife 's got damn good hands with a horse, too," he said gloomily.

It was a late party. At the door, Georgina put out her hand to me. "Good night. I saw you talking to George all evening." She smiled, obviously pleased; it was evident she thought I had been urgent in her defense. I should have let her think so; I should have kept silence; even as I spoke, I knew I should have kept silence. "Your husband," I said, "was telling me how very highly he approves of married women having careers. Writing careers, especially. He says such women should let *nothing* interfere – "

Georgina looked at me. She pulled her mink closer about her. . . . Somebody had lied. . . . It was an exciting moment. Standing before me, tall and lovely, was this a *vie manquée,* this poetess in mink? Whose the guilt, whose the fine fairy tale?

Small whips of scorn uncurled within me.

Merely another lady with a pose. Why did she do it, why did so lovely a creature feel it necessary to be misunderstood? . . . And then I had a surprise. Georgina's eyes were wide, blank and puzzled, like a little girl's eyes. She frowned, and color rose in her face. When she spoke she did not address me, but herself.

"Is it possible," she said, "that all these years I have just been *imagining* trouble?"

I went out and into the street. Love, I told myself tritely, causes many a mix-up. Or, had I been the target, the relief agent, of a long marital fight? But *still* I do not know whether, in this story, the tiger was the gentleman or the tiger was the lady. Which?

The following week the plot repeated itself, but with the moral, this time, in a very definite gender. This was a lesser party, much lesser — a musical tea party. A couple were introduced to me, plump, gray-haired, pleasant, and looking much like one another, with the comfortable resemblance that is the result of a long life together. "I heard you talking about music," said the husband, "about how it was a shame for anybody to give it up, and what fun it is to sing part songs. I used to sing. Barytone." He paused, glancing at his wife. Someone drew her away, out of earshot, and he looked after her. "I stopped singing years ago," he continued, "because my wife does n't care for music. Oh, I don't mean she *minds* it. I don't mean she ever *says* anything. I mean she just is n't interested."

Half an hour later, the wife came up to me, alone. She had a nice pink face and shy gray eyes. "I want to tell you something," she began. "Do you know, I 'd love to sing. I 've always been crazy to sing. I play the piano a little. But I can't keep on the tune very well, singing."

I assured her she could learn, easily enough. She could train her ear. But she made it clear, when she spoke, that what needed training was something far more difficult than an ear.

"My husband," she said, and blushed, "has perfect pitch. He 's at home most of the day. I don't dare to practise singing. It drives him – I mean, it would drive him crazy to hear me go off key."

Looking upon this shy and troubled person, I wondered again – a little wryly – if it be love that causes this confusion? All the same, I think it would be very trying to have a husband with perfect pitch. Once I knew a man who had perfect vision. He told me so himself, in the kitchen on our farm. Perfect peripheral vision, he called it. He was sitting across the table from me, drinking soup prior to his departure for other places, and he leaned forward and stared at me. "Looking straight at you like this," he said, "I can see everything on both sides of me, all the way back to my ears." He began to enumerate the things he could see. I never felt more uncomfortable; I do not know why, but I wanted this man – he was nobody's husband – to get on with his soup and get away from there.

Does this same impulse visit, at times, that shy lady whose husband has perfect pitch? People with perfect anything should keep the fact to themselves. In this connection I look upon Jarvis Houston as the ideal husband. Jarvis is a doctor, head of a large baby hospital, and he plays the piano very well indeed, so well that he could, as perfect pianist, have made life miserable for an unmusical wife and for some half dozen less skillful fiddling friends. But he is a farseeing man, Jarvis; far-hearing, too. One night he heard his friends play a Brahms string sextet, and instant conversion took place. In order to play that piece Jarvis set himself, in his thirty-seventh year, to learn the viola. Last month I played the Brahms with him; not only did he play viola, but second viola. First viola was controlled by Mrs. Whitelaw.

Excellent person, Jarvis, to give up a piano which he played to applause and bury himself in the alto voice—in the second alto voice! He said to me when we were done, "What an enormous pleasure, to be playing, and yet to hear the other voices!" No wonder he married what used to be called a feminist, and no wonder they are happy. It is Jarvis's wife who sits under the lamp with a blue pencil on quartet nights, and who never says, "Dear, haven't you played long enough?"

I cannot help thinking it strange, the tenacity with which most people cling to perfect vision, or perfect pitch, or whatever perfection exploits their particular ego. Must one be thus forever on the defensive, even to the point of destroying the colleague? So very often I am forced to remind even the most modest, agreeable pianist, "One moment—I am here also, if you please! Two of us are playing this music; in fact, Mozart wrote it for two. Would you mind," I urge gently, "after the next pause, the next retard, not plunging on alone, quite without me? Could you bear just to look round, over your shoulder, and see if I am ready to go on, too?"

And I ache to tell this person that if she will listen to me, wait for me, play *with* me, there will be more than two of us, in that room. There will be, not three, but a third—that rich long voice evoked by perfect ensemble, that entity created, out of the many, as one. It is this one upon whom we call, who is responsible for our meeting here; it is this one for whom we search, and it is this one that will elude us utterly unless we can subordinate ourselves, straining our innermost ear to catch the modulations of that voice. . . .

But I do not say this aloud; my pianist would think me highfalutin, transcendental. I say instead, "Oh, damn all loud players!"

Singers are the worst offenders on this score — real singers, that is, with lungs, bosoms, larynges, palates, or whatever name the sacred engine takes. Ask a tenor to sacrifice that high A to the ensemble effect and he will look at you in amazement, as if you came out of a zoo.

But not so violists. Let it be said that violists, to their glory, are indubitably at the other — and higher — end of the scale. I have never known a violist who was not a modest man. Modest men and good musicians, all of them with a working knowledge of two or three instruments, most of them ex-fiddle players. And a knowledge of three clefs, simple as it may seem, is seldom to be found separate from an intelligent musicianship. Nobody loves chamber music more than a violist; that is why he learned his instrument. "I was n't good enough, on the violin," he will tell you. "I could n't play those high notes up by the bridge. There were always better players available. I never really broke into string quartets until I took up the viola." And he lifts his instrument lovingly from his knee and passes his hand over its broad, bold back. "Nowadays," he finishes, more to the viola than to you, "nowadays we wedge into *all* the Tuesday nights."

There is, however, more than this to the psychology of why the violist is a true musician. Viola playing is, in its own peculiar essence, discipline for the ego. In fact, it eliminates the ego, even the virulent malignant male ego – *in toto.* As far as ensemble is concerned, viola playing admits no exhibitionism, no showing off. (Neither does second fiddle, but that is another story.) It is not difficult for the violinist to learn to play viola acceptably; it is very difficult for him to master the instrument. A viola is more than a large violin; it has a different timbre, a different quality, and this quality is not to be brought out by mere exaggerated violin technique. What brings it out we leave to such masters as Monsieur Bailly, whose name is blessed not only by those who have heard him in the Flonzaley Quartet, but by all those environs of Philadelphia upon which he has loosed so many excellent and sorely needed viola players.

This is not to say your violist is unaware of his worth; any good artist knows, and knows in every cell of his body, that he is a good artist, but your violist is apt, happily, to keep the good news to himself and let his instrument, or his colleagues, speak. Approach a professional string quartet after a concert; congratulate first the violist, and watch the others grin. "Anybody," a violist admitted to me on such an occasion, "knows the viola is the backbone of the quartet" – and his three colleagues nodded rapid assent. It was not for himself the violist spoke, but for his instrument. Your violist has, as a rule, neither melody nor base; he is, as Jarvis said, in the middle of the music; he can hear everything that goes on. When he has the melody, it is heavenly; one asks oneself in awe, "Is the instrument itself responsible for such a tone, or is it the skilled *vibrato* of that left hand?" When the viola plays bass, the ensemble, lacking the cello's deep finality, has another quality, a strange, tremulous something that projects us at once into an unknown place, into a fourth auditory dimension, a fascinating Erewhon full of half lights, half sounds; of breaths, as it were, half drawn.

Very often, though the first fiddle is leader, the violist is mentor and balance wheel to the quartet.

Particularly as to rhythm. Violists are as infallible, rhythmically, as percussion players; they will countenance no slip-ups, no chopped eighth notes, no cheated rests. How often, playing first fiddle, feeling myself flounder, I have looked across the stand at my violist, and never has he – or she – failed me! Always the inclination of the head, the little emphatic nod to give the beat – one, two, three, *one* . . .

Possibly this perfection of violists will seem more plausible if I list an exception, although it is difficult to think of that Briton as an exception to any one thing because he was a living exception to everything. He was queer, as queer as a cellist. He simply could not comprehend a slow tempo and he wore, winter and summer, the thickest woolen socks I have ever beheld. His legs were short and he thrust them in front of him when he played; this was years ago, but I am still wondering how there was room for his ankles inside those gray-ribbed fortresses. His aunt in Scotland, he told us, knitted them for him. When he got off the beat I would endeavor to bring him back by emphasizing the first note of the measure; failing this, I would try to catch his eye, but he would have none of it. Then, as the other players grew restive, I would tap the foot and count aloud. When I resorted to this last the Briton would blush. Burn is a better word; he would begin to burn at the cheek, and soon his face would be red as fire. It was weeks before he finally, on one of these occasions, stopped in the middle of a measure, laid his viola on the floor, looked fixedly at me over the stands, and said, with deadly seriousness: –

"If Mrs. Bowen continues to count out loud I shall – by God! If she counts another measure I won't play another note!"

Once a friend of mine in a country town in Virginia received a warning from the telephone company. It read: "If the undersigned does not pay his bill, the telephone will be *summarily yanked out.*"

The two ultimata unite always in my memory: declarations conceived in defiant, dignified formality and executed with a snort of earthy rage.

There was a silence after the Briton delivered his challenge. Dr. Retinus, next to me, broke it with a sound between a gulp and a hiccough; Henry Jones, our cellist, who is a Quaker and dislikes conflict, looked at his shoes as if he had never seen a shoe. The Briton picked up his viola from the floor, put it to his shoulder, and said, "Rhythm is to be felt, not counted. Let us go on with our music."

We obeyed as in a trance – all of us, that is, but Henry. Turning his blue eyes upward to the picture over the mantel, – it was "The Stag at Bay," – he murmured, "Hail, Britannia!"

Strangely enough, the Briton who roared thus loudly was, in all things but music, a man more modest than a mouse; he was small and thin, and his wife, an excellent pianist and peerless sight reader, was even smaller and thinner. What they did in the daytime, how they wrested from a hard Yankee world coppers sufficient to feed their small wiry frames, I know not; vague references were heard concerning Manchester and the Boot Market, but I asked no questions because questions, obviously, were not invited.

He was a musician, this Briton, and it is true that rhythm should be felt, not measured with a vocal yardstick. Counting aloud is an irritant; but, perversely enough, the only persons I have seen truly irritated by it are those who cannot – consistently cannot – keep time without it.

If violists are slow to rouse, they are, brought to bay, more dangerous than any ten-fingered, two-fisted pianist. Otto Lieber, of a famous symphony orchestra, one of the most thorough musicians I ever met, generous beyond measure to the insatiable amateur, will always be remembered by his friends as the possessor of a gentle nature; but once I saw him raise his antlers, paw the earth, and charge his enemy to the ground. One summer in Maine we went to a singer's house to rehearse a Chausson soprano song with string-quartet accompaniment – Lieber with his viola, my niece Cynthia, a professional cellist, and myself. It was the most unlikely room for music I have ever beheld, and I have beheld many. This one was all gilded – gilt chairs, gilt table, gilt curly picture frames enclosing blue Madonnas. The first chair I sat in gave way at the legs; the next, which had a pink brocade seat, gave way at the seat. The seat simply slid off, carrying me with it. Lieber, who had watched these manœuvres in his usual mild silence, shrugged his shoulders and went over and sat on the sofa, tucking his instrument benignly under his chin. (That afternoon was also memorable as the only time I ever saw a fiddler play on a sofa, particularly a short dark fiddler on a pink and gold sofa.)

The soprano hostess made sounds suitably apologetic, we murmured sounds suitably deprecatory; the soprano said, *"La, la, la,"* up the scale, and we were launched. My brother John was present, having hurried up from a Boston lawsuit to hear how the Chausson would sound. He is a big man and did not sit down at all; he leaned on the piano – but he did not lean long. At the fifth measure he began to grow restive – how well I knew the signs! Our soprano was out of time; she was taking liberties, and as the song progressed she took more liberties and more. Futile to follow her; there was no sense to what she did. Three of us clung as closely as possible to her voice; Cynthia, who is sixteen, went blithely on by herself along lines previously laid down by John at home.

"Ha!" said John, or something like "Ha." Anyway, it stopped us. John was glaring at the singer; I caught his eye and shook my head, my finger at my lips. I had seen John before, with singers. He put his hands in his hair and tore at it, but he was, for the moment, silent.

"You go too fast for us, Madame," Lieber said mildly. He got up and, walking to the piano, instructed her patiently, pointing to the notes with his bow. "So – this is a retard. A long, very beautiful *ritenuto*. We must all slow up together, yes?"

"But I can't *breathe*," the soprano said. "If you slow up like that, where shall I breathe?" Her voice, which had been plaintive, became a little sharp.

"Breathe!" John said, letting go his hair. "You singers, always thinking about breath! Always thinking about the divine epiglottis, or whatever, instead of thinking about the music. . . . Ha!" He caught my eye again and was silent, his eyes flashing fire.

"Let us," said Lieber softly, "try it once more."

We tried it once more, and once more again, and always wrong – always the beautiful slow retard, the tempered, balanced dying away, ruined by Madame's desire for a triumphant, high soprano scream.

Finally even Lieber laid down his instrument. "Madame," he said, "see how a fiddler breathes, with his instrument. So – " And he played two long bows, so skillfully united that the break was scarcely perceptible. "Can you not sacrifice a little, a very little, of the vocal effect to the music? Chausson wrote the music; we must speak it as he spoke."

Madame's lips went together tight, and came open. "You instrumentalists," she began, "simply do not understand about breath – "

"Breath!" John roared suddenly. "Bah!" He brought his fist down on the piano. "In not so many years," he told Madame, "you will not be breathing at all, and nobody," he looked at me and looked hastily away, " – nobody will give a hoot."

Silence. Cynthia near to tears of embarrassment, Madame speechless, the cellist grinning. Lieber, this gentle man, this pure musician, leaned forward and spoke. It was the first malignant thing I ever heard him say, and the last.

"But I – " he said, "I will give a very loud hoot."

CHAPTER VIII

On cellists, wild and domesticated

THE title of this chapter was to have been, "Are Cellists People?" But the instant I saw the phrase in type, I knew it was wrong – misleading entirely. Too smart, too sharp. If one wishes to give the essential definition of "cellism," to draw the especial mark which brands the intimate marrow of every cellist, one wields no smart and stinging pencil. There is about your cellist a softness, an engaging, inevitable good-nature; would he, else, contract for a lifetime of subways, trolley cars, street crossings, in company with that elephantine bundle? Watch a cellist tuck his instrument under his arm on a snowy night; hear him declare cheerily that he does n't need a lift, the El goes right by his door – and you understand that here is a soul tuned, not to fortitude, but to something more beguiling than fortitude. He simply does not *mind* the snow, he has a dreamy delightful impregnability to snowiness. . . .

"As queer as a cellist" is no idle simile. Cellists

are not to be accorded a like treatment with violists and violinists: when a stranger tells me he plays viola, I welcome him to my bosom with loud cries. I am apt to suggest that if he catch the 5.45 from town on Sunday night, he can be at our house with his viola by 6.10. Not so with fiddlers. Of the stranger who says, "I play the violin; I should like to play quartets with you," I am wary. The world is full of indifferent fiddlers; before giving them a definite invitation, I look them up; I investigate their musical credentials. It is a serious matter to be saddled all evening with a bad fiddler. John says he knows how to manage them; I have seen him managing them, and I am not so sure. His manner seems to me a trifle abrupt. He simply rises from the piano, says, "Well, well!" with enormous heartiness, and, "Have something to smoke?" . . . and then puts the person in a corner of the sofa "while the rest of us," says he, "just try over this new batch of piano quartets that came to-day from the library."

This method is not, however, at all effective with cellists. Cellists, as a class, are almost impossible to crush. Can this be due to their essential, unassailable guilelessness? When I meet a new cellist I am as wary as a fox, and when one does come to the house I am much easier if he be there at John's invitation, not mine. Last Sunday night I went down three steps into John's music room and found not one new cellist, but two, male and female. The male was already seated at the stands, his coat off, tuning John's big Bergonzi; the female, with auburn bangs, long earrings, and a tight, slim, black satin dress, was standing in front of the fire with her cello, spinning the instrument round and round upon its peg. "This is Mr. Breeze," John told me. "He 's the chemist from Alabama who 's come to testify in my big case." John looked toward the fireplace and back at me, unsmiling. "Mr. Breeze has brought his sister. She plays cello, too."

The back of my neck began to feel a little cold. I looked nervously round for Sarah, who has a merciful way with bad cellists. "Sarah 's gone to bed with a cold," John said gloomily. "Miss Breeze, what are you doing? Come on, we 're going to play the 'Forellen Quintet.' "

Miss Breeze was not disturbed. "I am warming my cello at the fire," she replied, "and I do not know that quintet." She had dimples, and a Southern accent. My niece Cynthia was at the first violin stand; the "Forellen" is her favorite piece; her face was a reflection of her father's and I saw we could expect no help from that quarter.

As I tuned the viola I heard the usual modest argument about who was to play first cello – a species of music-room finesse with which my brother has no patience whatever. John was practising the *arpeggios* in the third *andante* variation; he stopped. "Whoever plays best always plays first," he said. "No other arrangement makes sense. Here, I 'll count you a measure for nothing and we 'll begin. One, two – "

The Breeze family scrambled to its chairs as if it were playing, not Schubert, but Going to Jerusalem. We played the first *allegro,* with all repeats, and then John rose from the piano bench and, darting to Miss Breeze, shook her warmly by the hand. "You play better than your brother," he cried, "and your brother 's a cracking good cellist. . . . I beg your pardon. I beg your pardon."

The lady's earrings tinkled, her dimples went in and out. "What for?"

John looked at me, and grinned.

"Oh," I said quickly, "my brother just thought you were too *pretty* to be a good cello player."

"That 's it," John said. "That 's it" – and went back to the piano stool.

I have had, in my life, much trouble with cellists. Trouble finding them – good cellists are scarce as charity — and trouble with them when I found them. I made a list, entitled, "Cellists I Have Known." I got as far as seventeen and then I began forgetting their names, remembering only their wild hair, or the cut of their shoes. (These things are apt to be memorable in cellists.) Among the seventeen are two professionals of the first rank who are dreams of punctuality, steadiness, and those qualities defined by not forgetting to bring the music, not forgetting a music stand and rosin, not having a fidgety wife on the sofa, or a fidgety wife at home requiring premature departure and the stranding of the three other members of the quartet, not fussing about tender finger tips after a month's absence from their instrument. . . . Sarah, who has in her time entertained many times seventeen cello players, would have me add another "not" for cellists. Not, she says plaintively, with suspenders when they take off their coats to play.

I tell Sarah she is very provincial about this. Merely because her husband flops about the house, one hundred per cent American, in a belt and his shirt blousing out, is that any reason why other gentlemen should not appear snug at the circumference? To which she replies that it may be so, but, all the same, suspenders do not become her music room. "In my music room," she repeats quite plainly, "suspenders simply do not *go*."

Sarah's music room is, in truth, very beautiful — and it is Sarah's room. A music room and music are more closely allied, more pleasantly or unpleasantly interdependent, than any mere architectural blueprint could reveal. If John and the rest of us supply the string music, it is Sarah who has supplied the room, a room without which we should indubitably continue to supply music — but indubitably also with far less enjoyment and ease. It is a long room, wide and lofty; as we play, the notes rise and hover and lose themselves in the ceiling. Firelight leaps high under the huge chimney, and across long windows red velvet hangs in warm folds; Brahms and Beethoven look darkly down from the walls. Lights are attached to the wooden orchestra stands, chairs are high enough so that fiddlers' knees do not meet their elbows; the two grand pianos are always in tune, and along the south wall are oaken cabinets where music, cellos, fiddles, can be put to bed at night. And in the whole long room, not one uncomfortable chair. . . . No wonder Sarah, who created this paradise, is fussy; no wonder she makes rules: "Violins, bows, and cases not to be left on chairs. Chairs are here to be *sat* on. Cellists please put their cello pegs in rugs, as provided, and not in my oak floor."

But I will say this for Sarah: her severity applies only to the future, the probable – it is warning, not reproof. When rules are broken, when cello pins actually mar the floor, she makes no sign. She sits in her chair under the green lamp, causing roses to grow on a needle tapestry, and she says, "Play the *andante* again."

I wonder sometimes if Sarah's severity, like the housekeeping severity of many women, exists not so much for her protection as for ours? Does some sixth wifely sense tell her that John *likes* to have someone else than himself responsible for a sound show of decorum? I have my suspicions. In her heart of hearts, I think Sarah knows suspenders are as intrinsic to cellists as cellists are to her music room.

Glancing at the original notes for this book, I came across the following entry: "Most violists are excellent musicians and most cellists" – we have it again – "are crazy. Prove, by example. Daisy."

But I am not going to do this. I am not going to prove anything by Daisy, because I like her. She is young and pleasing; she is about the same size as her cello. It is true that the first time she came to the Hill to play with us, Daisy forgot to get off the trolley and rode all the way back to town, and it is true she sends occasional notes to Dr. Retinus with hearts entwined cut out of the note paper. But it is also true that she found her way back on the next trolley and played very well, and as to heart-shaped holes in note paper, I can think of more sinister things. Dr. Retinus says Daisy makes a mistake to roll her stockings below the knee; he says, indeed, it is a mistake any lady cellist might make once too often. . . .

All the same, I think I had no right to invent such a generalization in my notebook concerning cellists. Nobody likes to be put in categories: he is a transcendentalist, he is a typhoid carrier, he is a cellist. Cellists are not only cellists, they are human beings – all too human, Sarah would say. I shall not soon forget the time I secured an excellent cellist for Sunday night, and told Sarah his name. "Smith?" Sarah said, and at once looked very queer. "Not *Ellicott* Smith?"

"The same," I replied in triumph. "The best amateur cellist in the state of ——."

Sarah's face set stonily – a strange expression, for Sarah. "I am sorry," she said, "but I cannot have that man in my house, cellist or no cellist."

Sarah, at that time, was president of a large organization for the shelter of stray babies. It seems that the name of Ellicott Smith had but recently been linked inextricably, damningly, with one of the babies, and Sarah had officiated at the hearing. . . . I went home. "What shall I do?" I asked my mother, who is always interested in our Sunday nights. "I cannot telephone this man and say, 'Leave your bad morals at home in a coop with the baby, and bring your cello to John's house incognito. . . .' "

My mother has extremely strict ideas concerning stray babies—concerning, indeed, stray behavior of any kind. And she is, as I have said, eighty years old. Her answer surprised me. "A cellist?" said she. "If Sarah expects to find many cellists *without* stray babies, she will have a hard time."

This is not to say that cellists are, generally speaking, dangerous fellows. I have known cellists of the extremest domesticity. Henry Jones, for example, plays with us on the Hill every Tuesday night; it used to be Thursdays, but on Thursday Henry always came half an hour late; it was maids' night out and he stayed home to help his wife with the dishes. Henry is very pleasant to play with because he is so good-natured; what stamping and shouting occurs is done by Dr. Retinus and

Joe Knoedler, and by myself. One night the cello score had a particularly graceful phrase, repeated again and again. Henry played it correctly, but that was all. We began to fidget. "Henry," said Dr. Retinus, "don't play that figure the same way every time. You must differentiate your phrases."

Henry shook his head. "Can't. I 'm not musical enough."

We were completely disarmed. . . . Henry has one lamentable weakness. He likes to play in dance orchestras, and does, and, although he tries to hide it from us, his cello betrays him, of a Tuesday night. "Listen to him slide!" Dr. Retinus will say with a snort. *"Ouoiee, ouoiee, whooop!* . . . Disgusting! Henry, why can't you keep away from this syncopated business?" The other night I told him, sharply, "Don't drag out that first note in the measure. Let go of it. You 're not a saxophone. You 're a cello." Henry nodded, shamefaced. One minute later I found myself shouting at him. All three of us, as we played, were shouting at him: "Don't slow up. . . . *Cello!* You 're too slow!"

Henry stopped playing and looked up mildly. "Did anybody say I was too slow?"

The Chinese, I have been told, are taught to accept reproof gratefully, with a smile. I think

Henry Jones is the only cellist in the world with Chinese blood in him. But, like other cellists, Henry is erratic in his playing. I do not know why cellists are like that. The members of my household complain to me that every sponge cake I make is entirely different from every other. And why, they ask, when I always make them on Friday and always use six eggs? With the same group, the same surroundings, I have known a cellist to play gloriously one Tuesday night and horribly the next. In Dr. Retinus's music room is an aquarium full of fishes; pleasing blue lights illuminate the tank from within. At the sounds Henry makes with his cello upon certain Tuesday nights I have wondered the fishes did not freeze, the lights turn red. . . .

One summer evening, at Sandy Island, John and a lady cellist and I were playing trios, when the doorbell rang, and there was Henry with his cello. Henry does not belong on Sandy Island; in some thirty-odd summers, I had never seen him in that damp and salty place, so bad for cellos. He said he had driven a long way to get here, that I had told him we had a pianist on the island, but nothing more. He looked at the lady cellist and back at me, his blue eyes reproachful, then he laid his instrument against the wall and sat down. "I will listen," he said. "Go right ahead; I *enjoy* listening."

John made a sound in his throat. "Is that why you brought your cello a hundred and forty miles, because you like to listen to other people play? . . . Don't talk to *me,*" said John, "about what fun it is to be audience." He got up from the piano and called through the verandah door to his daughter. "Cynthia! Come in here. We 've got two cellists for the 'Forellen Quintet.' "

One rainy night a father, driving the family car up the family driveway, instructed his young son, "Hop out, Jacky, and open the garage doors." When the doors were rumbling comfortably back, the father, who had three children younger than Jacky, turned to me. "Is n't it marvelous," he said with a sigh, "is n't it simply unbelievable when they stop being in bed with colds and get old enough to be of some use?"

I tried to tell this story to John, apropos of his calling so confidently upon Cynthia and her fiddle, but John only looked at me in surprise. "Help us out?" he repeated vaguely. "By playing the fiddle?" But what, his tone implied, would a young girl do with her life if she was n't ready at all times to come in off verandahs and tune up a fiddle?

Henry Jones, observing these phenomena, remarked that he wished he had been brought up in a family like this one. He, it seems, had had to take his music by stealth, as a modern boy drives a car unlicensed, or hides his cigarettes in the garage. Henry's family, devout Friends of the old school, had linked fiddle with Satan; they sent their son to Southfield School, where, in company with some two hundred other young Friends, he was constrained to lead a fiddleless and godlike life. The third time he was caught in the barn with a violin, Southfield expelled Henry from its midst. Whether in his manhood he took up the cello from sheer bravado, because it was bigger, noisier, and therefore wickeder than the violin, I never asked him, but I was present, happily, when Henry had his revenge. Southfield has latterly, like other Quaker schools, turned quite furiously musical; it wanted a quartet to play for the children and Henry said he would bring one. When our Tuesday-night organization agreed to go, there was a glint in Henry's eye, and there was even more of a glint when we got there. Except for one palsied teacher, not a soul of his generation was in Southfield School that night and Henry knew it, yet he carried his cello through the halls with a swagger beautiful to behold, and as the four of us mounted the platform his face shone with a grin victorious. He made a little speech to the audience. He said he returned here, he returned here as a shining example of the ultimate triumph of . . .

Queerly enough, I cannot remember of what. Triumph of music, I wonder now? Of art? Or, more succinctly, of Henry Jones?

Once I sat upon a concert platform with two French horns and a harp, waiting to play the Brahms "Horn Trio" and to sing the "Harfenlieder." It was in an Elks' Hall, an enormous place, confusing because of the echoes. The horn players, professionals from a symphony orchestra, confused me further by referring always to their instruments as "those pretzels," with repeated offers to feed them to the stuffed elk at the door. . . . Cellists also bespeak their instruments casually; Henry Jones calls his the seal pen. When I was a little girl, this flippant relationship between cellist and cello used to distress me; at that time I looked upon all fiddles as magic, and one does not speak lightly of magic, nor take in vain the name. When I was about thirteen I played in a small orchestra with a great tall boy named Lowell Otis; he invariably referred to his cello as the dog house. Even in the ordinary course of rehearsal it was easy to see why, but I did not like it. I said so, demanding rhetorically, "Why do you have to go calling your cello a name like *that?*" To which he and his instrument made instant response with a series of growls, grunts, roars, and barkings of a virtuosity incomparable and convincing.

I played with a man, once, who had made his own cello, and he called it by no name but its own. He was, he said, an architect by profession, and I thought: A man would have to be, to make a thing as big as that. It was the only cello he had ever made, but, miraculously, it was a good one, graceful to look upon and responsive to the bow. I watched this man play with friendly envy in my heart, for I knew his was a double pleasure I could never experience – an unrivaled intimacy with both instrument and music. I have lived with my fiddle twenty years, in sickness and in health, in fair weather and foul. I know what to do when it has a cold, I know what it considers decent treatment, and I know what makes it balk and buzz and talk angrily to me, but I can never know my fiddle as Mr. Shaw knows his, who has fashioned it from stem to stern. Compared to his, my darling is but a stepchild.

Cellists have various private ways of confusing

an audience. Pablo Casals plays a cello with his eyes closed, and we rejoice only that he plays at all; in lesser cellists this trick has been known to cause instant death from missiles heaved from the gallery. The swaying cellist does not annoy me, but he drives other listeners to fury. Excessive swaying in any fiddler is distracting and engenders a suspicion of pose, ultra-temperament; I myself was reared in the old school which places a china plate under the right foot of every aspiring fiddler so the victim cannot sway, but must needs remain perched horridly upon an exhausted left leg. . . .

A friend of mine went to a cello concert in Paris where the performer rocked in his chair like a lightship. Wider and wider grew the diameter of his sweep, until a voice from the balcony called mildly, without rancor: –

"Mais, repose-toi, mon enfant! Repose-toi, pour l'amour de Dieu."

CHAPTER IX

Family music and roads that lead home to it. With an account of some musical battles, rebellions, and seductions, and a mention of Camilla's cello and the little raw fiddle

It has become an irresistible temptation, with me, to ask musicians by what road they came home. Some, like Henry, achieve music by rebellion; their innate musicality flourishes upon negation; a wall to kick against, far from breaking their shins, only fattens their artistic marrow, strengthens their artistic muscle. Patience, my little Quaker pupil, is like that. Once I abandoned her altogether. "I cannot teach you, Patience," I told her, "because you do not learn anything." After some months she called me on the telephone to ask if I would object to her playing for assembly, at school? She had, she assured me, been practising; the violin did not sound badly at all, and would I like to hear her play "Cinquantaine" some day? Tuesday, perhaps, at her old lesson hour?

"Cinquantaine" emerged from under her bow

with an actual lilt – the first lilt ever achieved by Patience. She must, in her vacation, have practised her fingers callous; I sat down and pondered, but I knew I should never dare this method with a soul less hardy than Patience. Not every fiddler has a Quaker genius for stubbornness.

Every year, on Cynthia's birthday, Anton Horner comes to play the Brahms "Horn Trio" with Cynthia and her father. For twenty years Horner played first horn in the Philadelphia Orchestra; it was Cynthia who asked him how he happened to choose his instrument. "Oh," he said, "for the same reason every German boy in my day wanted to learn the horn. We all had to be soldiers, sometime, and the army brass has a good place in the rear." But Horner's name tells his true story; his father and his grandfather and his great-grandfather were master horners. It is miraculous what Tony can do with a horn; he can sing you to sleep or he can march you to battle, but he says it was not always so. His father had to beat him to make him practise; he used to be locked in his room, first with a violin, then with a horn. "That's the way to do it," Tony said, looking benevolently round at our family assortment of young fiddlers. "Keep 'em at it, whether they like it or no!"

We used to be afraid to "keep 'em at it," afraid of our own parental enthusiasm and the possible mistake of overemphasis. How much music could be pushed down a child's throat without fatal indigestion? But we fear this no longer; we have seen our young revolt; around the piano of an evening we have mourned the loss of one child and another from the fiddlers' ranks – and then, eventually, they have come back. All but one, and him we await with confidence.

Even Cynthia tried to desert us – tried passionately, when she was fourteen. She practised with a scowl upon her face. "What good does music do me?" she asked me one day in fury, holding her violin at arm's length as if it were a serpent and would bite her. "Playing the fiddle won't get me into Omega Tau. It won't get me partners at dances. It just interferes with all those things. I *hate* music. What good can music do me?"

Nobody in her senses would try to put off a young and healthy Cynthia with middle-aged comfort, with "You wait. When you 're older, you 'll know." I hesitated, and Cynthia looked full at me. "You!" she said belligerently. "Aunt Kay, you play more music than anyone I know, except Father. I suppose you 've always been like that?

I suppose *you* never wanted to throw your fiddle in the sink?"

I never had, and no possible expediency of auntly compromise could make me say so. I felt suddenly, ridiculously, as passionate as Cynthia. "You 're spoiled," I said. "Put your fiddle in the sink and go sing Omega Tau. You 're not worthy of a violin."

And then I went home and tried to remember what it was like to be fourteen. . . .

At fourteen, three brothers flooded our house with members of the team (John had by then passed beyond teams). Large, muscular youths eyed my violin with curiosity, requested me to play upon it, and, as I played, lay dreamily upon their stomachs before the fire, smoking their cigarettes. Thus far, good. Song, melody, they could understand – but if I attempted to talk about music they fidgeted. They looked embarrassed and slunk away in search of easier game, of companions less intense, more comfortable. I saw this, – what girl could help but see it? – and I learned to keep silence when silence was in order. That I hated this restriction and rebelled against it in my heart made me no less the traitor. This was a decade before the word "highbrow" had been coined to crown the confusion of those whose blood leads them – flings them, willy-nilly – into embarrassing and lonely passions for Bach fugues. By the time that dread word was born, I was safe in music school.

Many a man who has known himself at ten forgets himself utterly between ten and thirty; I was fortunate in that my years of self-deception were short, my disloyalties brief. The largest of these took place, I remember, at Cynthia's exact age of rebellion – fourteen. There was a choice between playing in a recital at the Acorn Club, in Philadelphia, and going to a home-town affair called the Prep Dance. After weeks of musical preparation I told my mother I could not play well enough for the recital, I told my music teacher I could not endure the Wieniawski "Minuet," and I went to the dance. My teacher, who had come up from Philadelphia every Saturday for five years to give me a lesson, shook me from his list, spurned me eloquently in a letter to my parents, and I never saw him again.

Recalling these things, I wondered if all adolescents rebel against art, as they rebel against everything of parental instigation. If there were some way they could discover music for themselves, and not be pulled to it, sulking under the harness! Never to mention music, never to urge one's son to the piano – and then to have him come, suddenly and alone, upon beauty! Impossible; by the time his emotional apparatus was ready for music, his muscles would have grown too old to train. Horner was right; we have to keep them at it. . . . I have seen children pass through months of violent rebellion against music and months of warm devotion to it; the bridging periods of lukewarm tolerance are due, I think, to habit. Once in a while fortune aids the despairing parent by presenting the child with a new deskmate or roommate who can or cannot play, but who loves music. In the very nick, the very crack and needlepoint of time, Cynthia acquired a beau – transient as summer, but as welcome – who thought a violin more engaging even than curls, and said so.

I know not how it may be with genius; I have had no traffic with genius or even with superior talent; my children and my nieces and nephews are intelligent and ambitious, but without musical gift. No perfect pitch, no golden voice, no limber wrist of magic is ours for the showing; we exist merely as examples of how far the normal person may come into possession of music. Perhaps "average" is a word less offensive to the gods – do they, having created us in their image, look upon perfect pitch as the norm? However that may be, here upon earth I have found but one key to a child's heart, musically speaking, but one bait to which he will rise eagerly, repeatedly: active participation in ensemble performance.

How many mothers have said to me, "My little Freddy is only two years old," — or five or six, — "but I am sure he is going to be very musical because he will sit for *hours* listening to really *good* music on the radio" — or the victrola or whatever. With difficulty I suppress the reply, "Yes, my dear madam, and I have seen cretins in the asylum do the same for even longer hours, with the identical expression of sleepy wonderment displayed upon the face of your Freddy. And cretin and Freddy would enjoy the same sensation if stroked gently on either side of the backbone."

And this raises the question of cheap music, jazz, the radio, and all the competitions and comparisons that good music meets to-day. It is of no use to outlaw cheap mechanical music from the home; it is, indeed, dangerous. If the age decree jazz, let our defense lie not in prohibition but in education; let us teach the young to differentiate, to know that "Hello, Beautiful," however tickling to the palate, bears no more relationship to music than does soda pop to vintage wine. Verbal persuasion is unwise; exposure, repetitive exposure, to good music is what turns the trick; but the exposure must include more than listening. Children – I cannot say it too often – cannot prove things in the abstract; they think with their bodies. Do not ask them, therefore, to listen to Haydn; ask them to play Haydn, no matter how unskillfully. Children are savages – more difficult still, they are savages thrust by us into a sophisticated society, and they have prepared for themselves defenses against this society. Tell a modern child that Beethoven is beautiful and he will not believe you – until he has proved it by the repeated testimony of his own finger tips.

Cynthia has a victrola in her room; often, passing her door, I have heard her caroling to the tune of "A Dream Walking," or the most recent and appealing torch song. She invites me to listen. "Is n't that tune," she will demand, "simply divine?" But invite her to play the divine tune on her fiddle and she will turn up her nose. "Too thin," she told me once. "Those tunes, they 're boring to play." Cynthia still thinks Handel is boring to play, too. "It 's too *smooth.* Father, let 's do the 'Horn Trio.' There 's some *excitement* to Brahms."

I never saw a child that was not bored by soloism – his own performance as well as somebody else's. What boy wants to sit on a piano stool and play pieces for mother's visitors? He is shy and uncomfortable, and his resentment has a solid psychological foundation. A child detects instantly a false situation; in the name of music or culture or the acquisition of poise, he is being sacrificed to his mother's vanity; is it any wonder he only bides his time before flinging off music forever?

Once I had a violin pupil, a little girl of eleven whose talent was equaled only by her powers of resistance to pedagogy. A fond mother had set up a flourishing case of musical hatred ("Mother says music is beautiful as prayer, but I only practise because I get a dollar an hour for it"). One day I asked Mary if she would care to come to our house next Sunday evening. She eyed me suspiciously and asked if there would be music? I said no, that there would be some children her age and we might sing a little. "There will be," I said, "a string quartet and you can double with Cynthia on second fiddle if you think you can keep the place. But nobody has to play. We just do it for fun."

At home the bets were five to one against Mary's arrival, but on Sunday the stroke of six announced her — silent, very much on the defensive. She refused to take part in the singing and wandered about the room with a fine show of indifference, but from the corner of my eye I saw her pause by the fire and reach up a furtive hand to touch the old French horn on the mantel, saw her pause again to pluck a string on the cello in the corner. When we stopped singing she had come to anchor by the cupboard which holds the fiddles. "Is this the Maggini violin?" she asked. "That boy," nodding coldly toward John Junior, "sang off key."

Quickly, before John Junior could pick up this gauntlet, I replied that yes, it was the Maggini and we were going to play a Haydn quartet. I told her I was sure she would be wanting to go home before we began. Avoiding that sharp childish eye, "Will you please," I said rapidly, "get the Maggini ready for me while I answer the telephone?"

I left the room. The telephone had not rung and my lie had emerged from the larynx in a silly falsetto; did Mary know I was playing my last card? When I came back she was sitting comfortably before one of the quartet stands, John's Maggini on her knee. "I tuned it," she said, "and I dusted off the rosin. It sounds fine on the G string. I 'll stay if you 'll let me play it."

Even very small children love to handle a violin; its glossy smooth surface, the vibration of its plucked strings, exercise the fascination — but in superlative degree — of a perfect conch shell found upon the seashore. I honestly believe the privilege of dusting the Maggini has won more childish converts to music than many an endured symphony concert. All the radios in the world playing "Cock-a-Doodle-Doo," all the tickets for all the Youth Symphonies, would not have availed against Mary's rebellion. . . . Perhaps it is not so complicated as this. Perhaps any two-legged, deep-hearted creature fashioned by the Lord, if he held a fiddle in his hands, would know beneath his chin a cold emptiness, would itch to unfurl his right elbow in the balance of a long, strong bow.

This exercise of musical participation cannot begin too early. Let the child sing nursery rhymes with his mother, turn pages for the pianist as soon as he can read music, or sound A for the visiting fiddler to tune. Also, it can do no harm to leave the nursery door open when there is music. Music that drifts upstairs to a child's dark bedroom possesses a peculiar potency. Going to sleep to music at night, waking to music in the morning — absurdly enough, these experiences are, in some unaccountable way, musical participation; they define music, for the child, as a thing natural and homely, as much a part of the day as breakfast, dinner, and supper.

There are people who hate radios, and people — I say it with regret — who hate pianos and violins. Most families possess a well-rounded example of each species, and this is something we melomaniacs must acknowledge or see our family music crash dissonantly into family dispute. We who practise upon the flute are so taken up with making a wrong noise into a right one that we forget the persons to whom even a right noise upon the flute is maddeningly wrong. But there is a way to solve this problem.

When my brother John built his new house the architect said, "I understand the main feature of this residence is to be the music room? That is why you are building the house?"

John shook his head. "I want a room big enough for two pianos and at least a hundred people in comfortable chairs singing Bach. That will be the music room. But that is not at all what you call the main feature of the residence, and it is not at all the reason" — he turned to me and grinned — "why we are building the house."

Over his blueprints the architect raised the

patient inevitable eyebrows of architects in conference with clients. "We had a music room in the other house," I explained, "and in the house before that, too."

Impossible for me to speak of John's houses in any but the possessive case, although I have never actually lived in any of them. A house in which one's fiddle and one's children's fiddles repose under the piano can be spoken of in no other case than the possessive. . . .

"In all of the houses," John was saying with a large gesture of impatience, "in all the houses we had music rooms. Pianos, fiddles, flutes – Lord, yes. But what good did it do us?" He turned to me again. "There was no place to sit downstairs except the music room or a library that opened off it with double doors. Every time we wanted to play, the family had to stop talking or roll those sticky doors shut or go somewhere else. When we had people for dinner we could n't play or sing because the Browns did n't like music. Wasted evenings," – his voice grew indignant, – "wasted Saturday afternoons. And as likely as not a batch of newly published trios just arrived from Breitkopf and Hartel's."

John's eye was gloomy with remembered wrongs.

"So what we want," I began helpfully . . .

"Is a retreat," finished the architect, "for musicians."

"Nothing of the kind!" John shouted. *"We* are n't going to retreat. We 're going to play music. It 's the audience that 's going to retreat. The people that don't play . . . Look here!" John's finger was on the blueprint. "You see those steps? Well, they lead up from the music room to the hall. I want that hall a mile long. I don't care how it looks. It can look like a public school or a hospital or a lunatic asylum – I don't care. Then away down here at the end of the hall I want a room, nice and cheerful, with books in it, and a fireplace. Card tables, easy-chairs – *anything* in it," said John, "as long as it has a door that will stay shut."

"With a keyhole," interrupted the architect, suddenly inspired, "on the outside?"

"That 's it," John said, in his voice a rich and eager satisfaction. "That 's why we are building this house."

Speaking practically, I know of nothing more fatal to the musical progress of a growing family than a piano in the common sitting room. Particularly if grandparents live in the house, or a husband who, however sweet-tempered, is not sufficiently interested in music to endure those loud bleating sounds produced by a piano under striving small fingers. Sounds even more excruciating can be achieved by beginning violinists. I myself battled with this situation until so lately as a year ago, when, against vigorous protest, I had the piano moved upstairs. I put it – hideous but well-used upright – into one of those rooms possessed by every sizable family and known by such titles as the sewing room, Aunt Eliza's (deceased) room, or Uncle Jim's (deceased) study. I did this in secret, when the children were at school and their grandparents taking their afternoon siesta. Three large, grimy, pleasant men appeared at my door and with astonishing rapidity took the piano apart and flourished it up the stairs. In husky Irish whispers they requested a duster and delicately dusted its insides until the sewing room was dim with dust, after which they put the instrument together again and, with no more disturbance than three sneezes, took their pay, grinned, and disappeared.

I may call this one of the two major strategic musical victories of my life. The other was achieved when I moved the radio into the kitchen. Radios in the right place are as welcome as pianos in the right place, but in the wrong place, radios are . . . Let me tell a story.

On a boat going from Philadelphia to Boston I met a large genial man of middle age. He was the kind of man who carries a heavy elaborate camera and takes pictures of everyone on the boat – the very person I should have thought would love a radio. Upon the second evening of our voyage, a warm, soft summer night, I put my children to bed and went forward to enjoy the stars. As I hurried along the lighted deck a spirited raffle was taking place in the main saloon, with three radios as prizes. No one was on the bow deck; I stood alone by the rail thinking with satisfaction of my children tucked into starboard bunks and my automobile tucked into cavernous places below deck. Broken water slipped gently, monotonously past our bows; a mild contented revery possessed me, and I wondered why all the people who must go from Philadelphia to Boston in summer, instead of screaming through the night on heated wheels, do not tread thus softly upon the starlit wave.

A voice at my side said, "What more could anybody want?" – and I recognized the camera man. "Why," he continued, "don't people who have to go places remember about boats – and why are n't you down there buying chances on radios?"

I inquired if the gentleman so much wanted to win a radio, and he replied with gusto that he certainly did. To which I asked a little wearily *why* he wanted to win a radio?

He turned on me quite ferociously and said with a bitter, startling distinctness, "So I can carry it up here and drop it over the bow." His voice was exultant. "So I can watch myself drop a radio, brand-new and shiny, over this rail – splash! – into that black, irrecoverable grave. Into that bourn," he continued with a large gesture, and with magnificent disregard of the triteness of the quotation, "from which no traveler . . ."

"Returns," I finished, and extended my hand. He shook it gravely, and we resumed our starry watch.

It was that moment which told me Music in the right place is what domestic America needs – and it was that moment which, cherished all summer, inspired me to move our radio from living room to kitchen. The kitchen – is it not the hearth, the altar, the very sanctum of domestic life? Does it not deserve, therefore, as ornament, the very cream of modern invention? Also, is it not the room farthest from fiddledom and the piano bench? Since that night, peace has graced our home.

To revert to the fascinating query, "By what road do men come to music?" I advise against asking this question of a singer. The answer lies too wide of the mark. Fate, or God, or the circumstances of heredity shaped Fiorella's vocal chords with a beautiful physiological exactitude of proportion: Fiorella opens her mouth and a lark flies forth. But, we may ask, what has this to do with music? Seven toes on each foot would lead home as surely. Many a Fiorella have I met with throat of bird, brain of wax, and heart of putty.

On the other hand, I have seen more converts made, more unbelievers brought to Jordan, by singing than by any other blandishment of the muse. I have watched Sarah lead in the baptized by the dozens, and I have admired her technique, which is compounded less of enthusiasm than of an unshakable conviction that anybody in the world, if he will open his mouth wide enough, can sing — more important still, that he will like it. Sarah herself learned singing long ago — wise Sarah, who would have been drowned, deafened, lost completely in the vociferation of husbandly *arpeggios,* the urgent fiddle strings of her progeny. She had no voice; she could not, indeed, stay on the tune, but ten years ago an idea seized her, and with Sarah an idea is *fait accompli* no matter how long the way. At that time, no one in the family sang; John went about in trains and buses with "Magnificats" and "B Minor Masses" under his arm, but he never sang. It had not occurred to him.

Sarah sat down and trained – not her voice, but her ear. She began with "Three Blind Mice." Eventually she induced seven other women to sing with her once a week, on Wednesday morning. After a decent interval they procured a professional leader; the chorus now numbers ninety members, few of whom ever miss a Wednesday. The chorus does not sing in public; its aim is to read the literature of choral music. Sarah is herself astonished at the direction in which the wind of music has blown her straws; John, whom one would surely never think of as a straw, has become as enthusiastic a singer as his wife. Sarah and he hold Sunday-night singing parties; sometimes twenty people come, sometimes a hundred and twenty. John takes off his coat and leads the chorus; Sarah sits in the front row, singing, and somehow her very presence seems to balance the affair. John has a very useful loud voice; while he conducts, he sings bass or tenor, whichever seems to need support at the moment. He does not know if the room is hot or cold; half of us could faint from exhaustion and John would notice nothing save an annoyingly reduced volume of sound. It is Sarah to whom we turn in extremity. "We have sung enough," she tells John. "We must rest awhile. It is time for supper."

Sarah and John are themselves surprised at the choice of persons who elect to sing with them. Professional instrumentalists of the first water, not to speak of singers. Magic flutists from the Philadelphia Orchestra, harp pluckers, fiddlers, and pianists of glittering fame sit modestly sharing a Brahms "Gypsy Song," a "Palestrina Mass," with a red-cheeked, golf-playing importer of sisal hemp, a singing grandmother, or somebody's nephew home from school for the holidays. . . . We sing from six to seven-thirty; then, conversing in whispers, – only the professional singers seem to know how to use a voice without losing it, – we have supper. After supper some hardy soloist entertains us until we are recovered sufficiently to sing again. Names of these soloists – no matter how renowned – never appear on the invitations, but only the music to be sung and the names of the composers. This leads to occasional misunderstanding. One day Sarah, hurriedly preparing invitations, instead of writing out "Beethoven, Opus 132," wrote at the end of the programme, "An early and a late Beethoven quartet" – phrases as familiar to musicians as "three-minute egg" to a cook. A group of people, arriving at nine, said they had come late because they were especially fond of Beethoven and understood it was to be played *later.*

To us it is a matter of enormous pleasure that our one persistent rebel-to-music, my nephew David, the real musical talent in the family, who in his teens definitely did fling his cello, so to speak, down the sink – David sometimes sings with us at these parties. David never talks about music; like my brother's friends when I was young, he would strangle rather than admit he likes it, but, an infallibly correct sight reader, he sits with the basses and breathes deep, and we pretend not to know he is there.

Sarah's peculiar method of learning to sing is, I think, what fascinates everybody; perhaps I had rather say, her very individual outlook upon the arts. Sarah was not reared, like the rest of us, in a school which lets go, which roars its enthusiasm, turns red in the face, and pounds its feet when pleased. Sarah takes art for granted in the same calm, extremely practical way that she takes life and dinner time.

One Sunday we were singing a Handel duet

with the children, and Sarah read the alto part at sight. John was playing our accompaniment; he turned and stared at his wife. "Got that D natural, by heaven, did n't you? Where did you learn to sing fourths? I never heard you practise them."

Sarah replied easily that she had learned them driving the automobile. "Every time I turn a right-hand corner I sing a fourth, and every time I turn a left-hand corner I sing a fifth. I 've been doing it for months."

Not a child in the room, upon hearing this, but wanted to try the vocal leap of one-to-four, with all its variations. Perhaps it is not art, that kind of effort, perhaps it is not even music. But it is a game, and a good game.

One winter afternoon another fiddler and I were playing sonatas with Pamela at her house in Bryn Mawr—old sonatas for two violins and piano. Tea was laid before the fire; between movements we snatched at buttered toast and conversation. Pamela was at that time a candidate for the state senate; present was an enthusiastic young man who had called to discuss political matters with her. His enthusiasm concerned not music, but the autumn elections, and what he wanted was *talk;* it was obvious he neither knew music nor cared to know it. As I played I could see him where he crouched by the fire, a look upon his face half exasperation, half puzzlement. What, he was wondering, is Pamela up to now? Why do these people fling themselves so violently from the attainable concrete to the unattainable abstract?

After an hour he got up and, walking over to us, stood watching closely until we played the last chord. We played it – bang! – with a ring and a smash, and all three rose laughing – I do not know exactly why – from our seats. The young man laughed too. "Well, I 'm damned!" he said. "It 's *fun,* doing that, is n't it?"

Fun! I remember one child who played second violin with us at home for years. "It 's fun," she would say, as she put up her instrument when we were done. "Mozart is fun to play. I had to count sixteen measures rest, and I got back exactly on time. And I 'll bet nobody saw my foot move, either." (Like the indignant Briton, this child – who was not Cynthia – belongs to the school which thinks rhythm should be felt, not tapped with the foot. Cynthia herself counts, she says, all *andantes* with her stomach.) "Let 's try a new Mozart, next Sunday," the child would say – and then one night when she was sixteen she laid her fiddle on her knee and looked at me wide-eyed across the stands.

A long adagio cadence trembled on the air; the child's eyes were bright, bewildered. "It's beautiful," she said softly. "That Mozart – why, it's beautiful."

The long road or the short, the straight or the crooked, – as æsthete, poacher, or as sportsman, – I care not how nor by what road men come home to music. I care only that they come.

Having sung, every Sunday night, with my children and my brother's children until we knew, as it were, every song in the book, I bethought me of those other children who have no aunts, fathers, and uncles to sing with them on a Sunday. Or rather, I did not bethink me – Sarah did. She told me of a bleak and windy place which called itself a Home for Friendless Children; I went there, and somebody in a starched dress said, yes, I could sing with the orphans next week.

The following Sunday I too put on a starched dress, and, climbing a hill of spectacular bleakness, traversed a barren corridor and found my orphans. We sat and sang – shall I call it singing? We sat and shouted "Sleep, Baby, Sleep," and "Winter Is Done," while the gale raged round the naked orphanage windows. I had never led a chorus; my bewilderment, upon confronting for the first time these thirty-five howling monsters, was extreme. I tried discipline, the firm voice, the sharp retort – but while it brought silence, it did not bring singing. I began to sense dimly that what orphans wanted was not discipline, but something else. So I wore one night, instead of a starched front, my prettiest dress to the asylum. "Oh, Mrs. Bowen!" they cried. "I like your dress. I like your shoes with them red heels. Listen, my uncle's getting me new shoes next Tuesday – "

They drew near; they touched with rough fingers my flowery dress, my satin belt with the bright paste buckle. "Mrs. Bowen," whispered small homely Rosy, "I like to sing. I think your buckle on your belt is beautiful." And she threw her arms suddenly around my hips and laid her head against my stomach. Her glasses slid off. I said, "Rosy, would you like to come home with me some Sunday, and sing with my children?"

Thus it came about that I ushered seven selected orphans into Sarah's music room one Sunday night. All seven arrived very nattily turned out in the latest fashion – gray kid shoes with spiky heels, little capelets upon the shoulders. Sarah, who had expected poverty and patches, looked at me in bewilderment; John grinned. The seven orphans, ranging in age from twelve to sixteen, –

small, spectacled Rosy among them, – sat stiffly upon chairs, their gray kid shoes pointing disdainfully at the piano. They said, "No thank you," to cake, and "No thank you" to root beer. Sarah looked at me in desperation. What, her blue eyes signaled, is wrong with this party? Is it going to die? Is it turning completely sour? Are we being, of all things, patronizing?

Then we began to sing. My two nieces sang, my two nephews, my two children, my brother and his wife. Two by two, like the friends of Noah, we entered into music, lifting up encouraging voices. But my orphans needed no encouragement. They sang, very loud and true. All seven burst into harmony. Three sang alto, four soprano. John looked at me in astonishment. For sheer volume, my orphans were outsinging everybody, even the fluty-throated Cynthia – even John. He swung round on the piano stool. "Well!" he said. "Well!" – and the party began. They washed down litres of root beer, these orphans; only crumbs were left upon the cake plate. "Sure, we 'll come again," they told Sarah. "Sure, we 'll have some new songs ready. You have some ready for us too, will you?" . . . "Yeah," added my small Rosy, "that 's it. Turn and turn about 's fair play."

And then they announced they wanted an orchestra. "The boys want it. The boys ain't got no music only Byron Heiser's trumpet and a couple of mandolins."

In three weeks I had collected enough instruments for an orchestra. I frequented stylish dinner parties, stylish tea parties, stylish anythings I could find. I said to my conversational partner of the moment, "Have you an old fiddle in your attic?" Day after day I took old fiddles to Mr. Moennig on Twenty-first Street and he strung them up, supplied bridges, pegs, cases. "No," he would begin cautiously, "I got no old cases in this shop and no old bridges and no old anythings" – and he would disappear into the cellar and come up again with two army cornets and a battered cello case.

Finally I had seven violins, two cellos, two cornets, a drum, two violas, two clarinets, five mandolins – and no soul in the orphanage that could read a note upon the musical staff. Mr. Lerando was induced to come upon a Wednesday night and give instructions upon not one, but all of these instruments. Mr. Lerando is a miracle. I led him up the windy hill to a room clamorous with orphans who had "signed up" for the orchestra. Forty-three of them, all talking at once.

"How," I asked Mr. Lerando helplessly, "will you begin? How would *anyone* begin?"

Mr. Lerando put his hands on his comfortably rounded hips and surveyed the orphans with his large, soft brown eyes. "First," he said, "I got to sort 'em out."

He did. What is more, he brought, the following Wednesday, what he called a helper, who sorted them even further. Each Wednesday, since then, I have taxied Mr. Lerando up that hill, and each Wednesday my respect for him increases. He has a high stomach and rolling hips, and he is extremely energetic in an Oriental way. He never jerks at things, he flows at them – simply rolls over them and around them until they are his. He is not at all afraid of orphans; I do not believe he is afraid of anything. "What we need," he told me one night as I sat upon an orphanage window sill watching him teach the cello to six perspiring boys " – what we need in this orchestra is a double bass."

"Gracious!" I said. "A bass fiddle? But they cost a hundred and fifty dollars."

He waved his hand. "Oh, I don't mean to *buy* one. Cer'nly not, lady, cer'nly *not*. I just meant, now, when you 're traveling round, if you should happen to run acrost one?"

I have "run acrost" all sorts of things, traveling round. Once in my Uncle Tom's roll-top desk I even ran across a mummied cat. But a bass fiddle? I told Mr. Lerando I was sorry, but I had a distinct conviction that unless my life emerged suddenly into far larger channels, I should never just happen to run across a double bass, and if he really wanted one we had better organize a campaign.

Only one thing seemed to trouble him, at the orphanage. "How," he whispered to me one night, "can I tell 'em, polite, not to come to cello lessons with those greasy hands? Look, look at this girl's hands now. Young lady, – Camilla, – look at this instrument, at the finger board, how the grease comes off you onto the strinks already! Is that nice now?" asked Mr. Lerando. "Is that right? Is that the way to treat a cello God gives you?"

Mr. Krupel, the helper, has a slightly different problem. Mr. Krupel teaches the violin. "Beets," he told me, waving a hand at the pupil, "are not good for fiddlers."

Having reared my children, with some trouble and expense, upon vitamins and roughage, I was surprised. "Beets?" I repeated. "I thought they were excellent." But Mr. Krupel was already unfastening the pearls from Gracie's neck. "Beets get in the way," he explained. "I must always" – he smiled – "untrim the ladies when they come to me for violin lessons."

One night Rosy appeared. "I got a vylin," she said. "I want to learn it."

She placed in Mr. Krupel's hands a tiny white violin, innocent of bridge, pegs, finger board, and chin rest. "Where," asked Mr. Krupel, "is all the warnish? Ach," he said, "Rosy, it 's just a little raw fiddle."

Once, in my youth, I stole from the wilderness a very small black tree and planted it in my mother's garden. It grew and spread and flourished, and one summer I asked the gardener, "What kind of tree is it?" He looked at it, frowning. "Oh," he said, "it 's just a little wild tree."

Absurdly I wondered, as Mr. Krupel spoke, if the little raw fiddle had been fashioned, perhaps, from somebody's little wild tree?

Every Sunday night when we are done singing, the orphans bring their instruments to tune, and this tuning must last until Thursday, when Mr. Lerando comes to the rescue. "Lady," they cry, "ma'am, you got the screw for my E string on you? You got a chin rest, half size, for Rosy? – Rosy, go get your violin; the lady brought your chin rest. Rosy, you *dumb?* Shut up your mouth hanging open like that and go get your violin. Don't you *want* no chin rest?"

Rosy flies. She comes back with the little raw fiddle which, strangely enough, has a tone bigger than all the other fiddles. A little like Rosy, this small loud raw fiddle which, when I draw the bow, makes itself felt in every corner of the bare, shabby room, trembling on the air, vibrating even after my bow has left the strings. . . .

Camilla was too small for the big cello. Camilla has hands you can see through, a wide red mouth, long eyes that turn up at the corners, and no kith or kin alive. Camilla needed a three-quarter cello, but even a three-quarter cello costs money. Twenty-five dollars, Mr. Moennig had said. "This here cello," Camilla told me, "it plays itself onto my backbone, like." She wriggled, grinning up at me under heavy, wild black hair. "That cello will shiver it more, Camilla," I replied, "if you practise. If you really work."

Camilla said nothing to this. But she laid her cheek against the finger board and rubbed it up and down. "Friendless Children," the sign read upon the gate. Looking at Camilla, I knew she was not friendless now. . . . The Board of Governors was to meet on Tuesday, and the Board, unluckily, was not interested in music. Could I entice from it twenty-five of its dollars? Without bombast or sentimentality, could I tell an unmusical Board how, for twenty-five dollars, a child might be given a friend for life – how, if she but learned the language, Camilla and her cello might converse in speech more eloquent than the tongues of angels, truer, less costly by far than the protestations of many friends?

I remembered Frank Gittelson's words, "Music is to be played, not talked about" – and Santayana's, "Music is not a criticism of violins, but a playing upon them." Yet Gittelson, when music needed a defense, had laid down his violin and turned to speech. And Santayana, has he not written whole books in defense of beauty? . . . Because of that adversary whose ear is deaf to any speech but words, because, for instance, of governing boards, there are times when a champion of music must do other than play.

On Tuesday the Board shook its head and smiled – and voted Camilla, to its everlasting honor, twenty-three dollars and fifty cents.

CHAPTER X

Country music, with an account of Sidney's hospitality and Felicia's, and an introduction to some Gilead choristers

WHEN we set out for Jamestown and Sidney's farm, my children and I wondered, concerning music. A month at Sidney's farm would mean, in all likelihood, science and silence and harvesting the beans – honorable occupations all, and pleasant upon a fresh salty hillside. Sidney's immunity to music is as extreme as his intelligence, and as interesting. Wearing his indifference upon his sleeve for all to see, when the fiddles are tuned Sidney walks away – but over his shoulder he casts a backward glance. Crusader that I am, I ask myself, at times, if Sidney's sudden shyness in the presence of music does not mask a fierce and secret hankering after such comfortable flippancies as fiddling?

Sidney's days are spent in a research laboratory called "the Building." What he does there he does well, with a patience and a passion quite terrifying to the uninitiated. It is natural that, outside the Building as well as in, such a man should reject with scorn the dabbler, the amateur. Dabbling – so pleasant for us whose blood simmers permanently at degrees ninety-eight – must seem, to a spirit more highly temperatured, as dangerous as sin, and as sterile.

I was a bit conscious therefore, upon arrival, of our three fiddles, all sizes – my daughter's small one, my own, and a huge viola, which last it is my habit to carry in case of emergency. "What emergency?" Sidney asked, lifting the fiddle cases from my automobile. A viola was not, apparently, the answer to any of his emergencies. I asked him please to tell me what would happen if three violinists and a cello player met up here in the woods some night and there was no viola available east of Providence? Violas were seldom to hand in summer. Sidney agreed gravely over his pipe that it was well to be prepared; for himself, he always took an extra gun on a gunning trip. . . .

I went into the house and saw, to my surprise, a piano. An upright, looking out of place, somehow – a little awkward, as though it were there on sufferance, and knew it. Sidney's wife had had it tuned; indeed, I felt immediately that she had caused it to be carried out from town for me; the suspicion brought with it mingled feelings of gratitude and guilt. So much trouble and expense to provide merely — *fun?* I turned to my host and hostess. "How," I asked, "will you put up with us for a whole month? Everything you do, all of you, you do perfectly, like professionals. Can you bear it, our dabbling at music?"

"Your what?" Sidney said. "If you call what you and John and the rest do with music *dabbling,* I should say you were dabbling up to your necks. One inch farther and you will all be as drowned as coral."

Satisfaction swept over me in a glow, childish and pleasurable. Sidney's wife, like Sidney, is a research doctor and cannulates with passion the lymphatics, but Sidney's wife I had not feared; I knew her, to date, as a person completely unmusical, but I knew also her quick smile and the fact that, being woman, she was made of tissue more yielding than man. Nevertheless I was gratified when she said, "You must invite your friends from the Music School to come here and play — what is it? — *sonatas.* Play your sonatas and we will learn what it is all about. It will be good," she added, "for Katy and Sally."

Katy and Sally are Sidney's children and they are far too competent to need anything that is good for them. Also the thought of music as being so definitely good for anybody rather terrified me.

But I invited what they called my musician friends to come to the farm, and everyone was very courteous and concerned. The first essay at music took place upon a hot July night, with the poplar leaves moving languidly outside, with moths flying against the screens and blond Hans at the piano, leaning slightly forward, his body swaying. Hans had on a blue cotton coat, clean but entirely shapeless, no shirt, a large green and red silk muffler round his throat, and a cigarette in his mouth. At supper Sidney had eyed this costume curiously; Sidney always said musicians were queer. "You are interested in my coat?" Hans had cried in his light, eager voice. He had leaped to his feet and run round to Sidney, holding his coat out by the tails. "Is n't it splendid? See – it has no shape. Simply no shape at all. I bought it in a sailor's shop in Göttingen."

"H'm," Sidney said, and I hastened to urge the splendor of the blue coat. . . . And now Sidney sat at the far end of the long room, sunk in shadow, as Hans leaned above the lighted keys. Sidney's head was bowed; how could I tell if he were sleeping or suffering, or if he were content? His wife sat in darkness near him and, because I know her well, I knew her brow was puckered, her dark eyes alert to learn what this thing was. ("If you love it so," she had said to me, "I must be missing something. Teach me what this thing is.") On the floor were Katy and Sally, stretched comfortably upon their stomachs. The music ceased and Hans turned to me. "Bach?" he said, and I nodded. He smiled toward the darkened room. "I shall play for you the 'Chromatic Fantasie and Fugue.' "

"What?" Sidney's wife said. "I mean, if you don't mind, what *is* chromatic? And especially, what is a fugue?"

"A fugue?" Hans looked at me in bewilderment. "She knows so much that I can never know, and she asks what is a fugue?" He was on his feet, gesticulating. "Here – I tell you."

He told them. Sidney remained motionless; Katy and Sally sat up, enchanted, like birds before a serpent. Suddenly Hans stopped talking, looked wildly at me, laughed, ran his hands through his blond hair, and hurled himself upon the piano. "Why did you let me talk?" he asked me afterward. "These people, so intelligent and so serious – one must not try them too far. They *work;* they make the world go round. And in heaven," he smiled, but his voice was grave, "they will have crowns outshining all the rest."

So the days passed, pleasantly enough, until on

the village street one morning Felicia hailed me, leaning from her car – Felicia, who I had thought was in Budapest or Cochin China. "Bring your fiddle to my house to-night," she called. "At eight sharp. We 're doing the 'Fifth Brandenburg Concerto.' "

The "Fifth"? It meant at least six good fiddle players. I jumped three times into the air, astonishing the local police sergeant. Felicia bent to the gear shift. "Where will you get a flutist?" I shouted. Felicia said, "What?" and I put my fingers to an imaginary flute. "Have you got one?" I yelled, and when she called back, "Smith!" I hugged myself with joy, for although I had never heard him play, I knew what Carleton Smith could do with a flute. . . .

Hans called for me in the blue Siegfried. I have always hated the facetious naming of automobiles, but Siegfried suits this large, bright, fearless adventurer. We sped through Eastown, down lanes, down country roads with fields darkening on either side. It was nine before we drove up Felicia's hill and, abandoning Siegfried, walked up the path. There is always a thrill in the approach to a strange house, and to-night was more than a thrill. Right out into the woods floated the "Brandenburg Concerto," measured, classic, precise; the sound of it steadied my heart into that strength Bach always gives. . . . We stood in the doorway, before us a great hall, dark-beamed, dark-paneled; seven music books upon seven stands, seven string players intent upon the notes, a piano in the corner with Bruce Simonds playing with the delicate precision that is his. There was Mott Shaw with his cello, that good cello he had made himself. There stood Carleton Smith with his flute, his long supple torso bowing and bending as he led the ensemble. There was somebody's sister – in what forgotten ensemble had I played next her yellow bangs, her incredible violet eyes? How, I wondered, could a creature of such fragile beauty hold a viola? And there was my chair, empty, the music open on the stand.

The movement ended, Felicia came forward, brisk and gracious and healthy in long white taffeta. I drew my fiddle from its case, screwed my bow hair to balanced tautness, rosined it sweetly, and hesitated, hovering round the eighth chair. I knew a moment's panic; what if, being late, I were not invited to take part? Felicia, tuning her violin, signaled me to sit down and play.

Through opened casement windows the fir trees were dark. The flutist nodded to me; I took the beat from him, watching him warily, for Felicia had put me in the first fiddler's chair. "Feel what I do; go with me," he told me wordlessly. Somehow, when we were really under way, when the uneasiness incident to playing in a strange ensemble was gone, somehow, sensing the fir trees so near, the wide country sky above the woods, there beat through my head the words of Brahms's "Requiem," "How lovely is thy dwelling place, O Lord of Hosts."

And once again a voice within me said, as it has said so often, Where have you been? You have been away, woman, and now you have come home. . . .

And then suddenly I saw a blank space on the music, with the number 63, and knew it meant – Oh, horror! – sixty-three measures rest. Would I find my way back on time, after that long journey? All seven of us had the rest, but, not being aware of this, I began to count, for safety's sake. The pianist played alone; I counted the entire sixty-three measures and not a beat did Simonds miss, although he played quite freely. And I was reminded of something Frank Gittelson taught me. He was at John's house one evening, teaching Cynthia, against his better judgment, to play a Beethoven sonata – he did not consider her advanced enough for Beethoven. The inexperienced player may jiggle gayly through a Haydn rondo or fling himself with recklessness upon a César Franck quintet and emerge unscathed – but Beethoven is not to be trifled with. Attempt to fake a Beethoven *andante* and, no matter how few or simple the notes upon the page, the blasphemer will come away scarred, baffled, and naming himself lower than Balaam's ass. But this is not what Gittelson taught me; Gittelson's lesson concerned rhythm. John was at the piano; Gittelson listened, leaning his back against the curve of the instrument. He shook his head and bit his fingers, and, thrusting his hands into his pockets, walked up and down. Then he took the violin from Cynthia.

"Listen now," he said. "I will play the first movement through, and I will play it very free. I shall not lose a beat. . . . You don't believe me? Very well, where is the metronome? You want to bet?"

He won his bet. Beautifully phrased, perfectly accented, lyrical and suave, the *allegro* progressed, and because the player was so sure, because I knew he would not lose a note, the tick of the metronome – so maddening to an insecure player – bothered me now no more than the beating of my own blood along my veins. He put down the violin and took out a huge handkerchief and mopped his forehead. "You see?" he challenged us. "Never a dull moment. That is rhythm." . . .

So, beneath Felicia's dark-beamed ceiling, the sixty-three "Brandenburg" measures unfurled themselves, rolled on lightly, gracefully, yet inexorable in their rhythm as the pace of doom. With those measures I marched the inevitable circle; my mind soared, wandered to Gittelson and Beethoven, but I must perforce come back on time – I could not help it. And there is in such rhythmic compulsion an enormous satisfaction, direct and sensuous; I do not know the reason, I know only that to unfold the rhythmic bow brings a delight and a fulfillment comparable to the drawing of one breath when another breath is done.

When the "Brandenburg" had sounded its last chord I returned to Sidney's farm, and the next day we took our three fiddles into the country. Real country this time, not a gracious series of gentlemen's farms along an easy road, but a rough Connecticut hillside attained after endless bouncing over sun-baked ruts. No telephone, no ice, no plumbing, no supper until the cows were milked – and no piano, tuned or sour, within miles. Here we remained until the autumn, and it was here I learned what country music means, learned that even the "Fifth Brandenburg" heard through fir trees is not truly country music. Gilead taught me country music; Gilead, where stony pastures slope to the brook, where tired city ears are soothed by the long sound of leaves blowing, by the creaking of wagon wheels on dusty roads, the sharpening of a scythe in the field beyond the wall. . . .

A violin in the country has a different identity than in town. It needs no accompanying instrument, but stands alone upon its own sweet dignity. One can dance merrily to a lone fiddle; on a Saturday night in Gilead I have stamped out many a lancers, a quadrille, or the Wild Irishman, my heart bursting with admiration for the waistcoated, coatless old fiddler who was sole orchestra. I could never do as he was doing; the notes – I could play the notes readily enough, but that jerky delightful rhythm, that chuckling Scotch syncopation – was it mere book learning, city sophistication, that had robbed me forever of the power to catch with my bow that contagious bucolic bounce?

One fact I discovered immediately. In Gilead, a woman with a violin is expected to play upon it, not for her own esoteric pleasure, but when the world demands. I found myself the only fiddler in Gilead township and as such my responsibility was not light. When the Children's Play upon the rectory lawn needed incidental music, I was the music; no apology was offered concerning the lack of a piano. The word "accompanist" was not so much as mentioned. Scared and lonely out under the trees, with nobody to sound A or nod my cue, I played madrigals, old dances, my accompaniment the rustling of the August corn in the rector's field – silo corn, taller than a man, bowing its long russet silk above the wall.

I was requested to bring my violin to church, and found myself obeying with astonishing regularity. I am no churchgoer, but each Sunday morning for many weeks my fiddle and I climbed those steep steps to the choir stall. Sometimes, when Mrs. Peaslee was late to arrive at the organ, I stood in the stall looking down over the church and played my violin alone. I never heard it sound so sweetly, or felt more sure, when I drew my bow, of the strong readiness of its response. It was my violin which introduced me to St. Peter's Church, and I am grateful for this introduction – anybody would be grateful. Low and squarish and set back from the road, St. Peter's is made of bricks painted white; the steeple rises no higher than the giant elms which shade it. Pastures spread on either side, and beyond the pastures are cornfields, marked, bounded by the low stone walls that are as indigenous to New England as the apple trees. Behind St. Peter's the churchyard slopes to a deep valley; here rests Eliza Greenleaf, "Spinster in the Sight of the Lord," and Captain Nathaniel Hastings, "Master of the Barque *Henry*." On August nights the moon, climbing above the western ridge of hills, lies upon the stones like a great sheet, white and washed and quiet. . . .

And on Sunday mornings when young Jonathan exhorted us earnestly concerning Hell, I, sitting aloft in the choir stall, my fiddle on my knee, was aware through arched, open windows of Jonathan's cows, clanking long, contralto bells. Once, cocking an ear to this slow melody, Jonathan paused. "That 's Hulda," he explained to the congregation. He nodded toward the window. "She 's into my corn. You, Ephraim Martin back there, just you slip out and lead her home. . . . And when Adam and Eve sought to reënter the garden," he resumed evenly, "there stood an angel with a flaming sword . . ."

I remember well his sermon on "the Fall," because it was that morning things came to a head in the choir stall. That morning a musical feud, long dormant, crashed into action on the very organ bench, but not until Jonathan had finished his sermon. He stood there, his huge shoulders hidden under a white surplice, his great hands resting on either side of the pulpit, and described Eden. Pleasant it was, he said, with all manner of flowering plants. Columbine and phlox and Canterbury bells. Everywhere flowers gave off their fragrance. As he was speaking, air drifted in from the fields. Lilies, had Jonathan said, or hay, newmown and fat with clover? Jonathan described to us how fruits hung on the trees of Eden, pears and apples, peaches and plums. . . . Right across the window by St. Peter's altar, branches reached, heavy with ripening fruit, fine young apples, hard and shining. . . . "And there stood an angel," said Jonathan, "an angel with a flaming sword . . ."

Mrs. Peaslee is always very nervous at the organ, but that morning she seemed unusually fluttery. When I came up into the choir stall she had run to meet me. "Mrs. Bowen, will you *please* – I mean, I don't know this first hymn and I hope, if I get off, you will just go *on*. . . ."

I assured her gravely that I would go on and *on*. Until I first tried fiddling in on all the Amens, all the plain songs, I had not realized how very complicated the Episcopal service really is, but I wondered this morning at Mrs. Peaslee's timidity, for she knew the ritual to perfection. I looked about for a possible source of her perturbation and found it. Miss Mamie was in the choir stall; she had climbed silently up and slipped glumly into her chair by the organ. Miss Mamie had been St. Peter's organist for twenty years; the previous summer she had abdicated, pleading old age, and Mrs. Peaslee had taken her place. But since then, unless for some reason Mrs. Peaslee was absent and Miss Mamie could have her place at the organ, the latter never set foot in church; she could not endure, she had told me, to hear the Peaslee play organ without any bass. It is true no Peaslee foot ever touched pedal; I myself had become quite used to the resultant clear, innocent treble, and I had put it down to Mrs. Peaslee's constitutional spinsterdom rather than to any lack of organ technique, for Mrs. Peaslee, though married many years, will carry forever that fluttery deprecatory something that brands its possessor as spinster. Under that prim foot, no masculine booming could issue from any organ.

Whereas Miss Mamie, at seventy-odd, with every right to spinsterdom, wears a red hat to church and plays the organ like a drunken sailor. One Sunday before this, I had played with her. She had stalked into the choir stall, flung one look at the hymn board, remarked, "Stuff! Wispy diddely

Peaslee tunes!" permitted Jonathan to announce them as per schedule, and had then plunged confidently into the virile song of her choice. To waltz time and to march time, with every stop out, we had rollicked through with a pedal roll, a booming of the kettledrums, and the congregation followed us with gusto. I never heard them sing so loud. I might add that Miss Mamie is short of build, with piercing black eyes under heavy brows, a magnificent topknot of abundant, gray-black hair, and that she moves slowly, with an immense and peculiar dignity. One of her admirers, who happens to be an organ builder, told me that when Miss Mamie sailed into a room he was instantly reminded of a thirty-two-foot diapason. . . .

Had I been Mrs. Peaslee on the organ bench, I should have been nervous too, with Nemesis four feet from my right elbow. Shouting hoarsely across her rival, Miss Mamie said she had come to church to hear me play *that violin,* and relapsed into a silence so glum it made us all uneasy. . . . As organ player and as human being, I much prefer a Mamie to a Peaslee, yet I found myself sorry for the latter because I knew that, if it came to the act overt, she had no chance at all. She would go down like so much chaff.

And she did. After the first verse of "Stand up, stand up," Miss Mamie rose to her feet and, leaning over Mrs. Peaslee, began pulling out the organ stops. Mrs. Peaslee's thin shoulders shuddered, her hands tensed on the keys, but she did not look round or miss a note. At the next hymn Miss Mamie sat down beside her rival and used both hands on the stops, remaining upon the bench when the hymn was done. During the Offertory Mrs. Peaslee, flinging me one appealing glance over her shoulder, led into what she always referred to as "the selection." The selections are derived from a well-thumbed booklet entitled *Appropriate Selections for Church Playing,* by Alfred Beam; Saint Peter himself could not divine on what basis, romantic or practical, Mr. Beam selected what he selected, but this morning it was Mendelssohn's "Spring Song."

I saw Miss Mamie seize the stops – full bass, contrabass? My organ vocabulary is hazy. Whatever she did, Darius's lions filled the church, Gabriel's trump screamed tremolo. I saw her reach out a powerful short leg, slide her foot over Mrs. Peaslee's beneath the organ, and I saw Mrs. Peaslee, pushed to the uttermost extremity of the bench, fall off and disappear. The lions, Gabriel, the *vox humana,* came together in a symphony of horrible magnificence, and the "Spring Song," changing suddenly to "Onward, Christian Soldiers," – Miss Mamie's favorite hymn, – became a roar of victory. Jonathan, who was engaged in prayer, looked up from the chancel steps in surprise, the congregation rose hastily from its knees to its feet and swept into song. . . .

The race is to the swift, thought I, fiddling away. In music as in life, the victory is to the strong. Over my violin I looked for Mrs. Peaslee; she was upon her feet, singing with the rest. . . . To the strong? . . . It is a good tune, "Onward, Christian Soldiers," a swift, contagious rhythm. . . .

CHAPTER XI

On organs and organists. Wherein Ernest expounds the true faith, and I explore strange territory, returning home with the sad conviction that only a giant may ride behemoth, and that ladies had best stay where they belong

WHEN I was a child of eleven I heard the organ play in Antwerp Cathedral, and went home and wrote about it in my diary. I have the diary here beside me. Words like "rumbling, roaring, glorious" – words I had read in a book. When it was loud it was "a thunderstorm"; when it was soft, "I looked up and I felt as if I was lifted from the earth and was flying and flying."

And when I was thirty I heard the organ play in Milan Cathedral, but I had learned by then not to try to put sound on paper. Vaguely I sensed that it could not be done, but only vaguely – until I met Ernest. Ernest is the first organist I ever knew, and there is nothing vague about him. Until I met him an organ was to me Gothic glory, or it was played in a theatre and was ridiculous.

It was Ernest who first seduced me from the cozy boundaries of fiddledom into this land of giant voices. It was he who taught me that an organ can touch many planes between glory and absurdity, and, above all, it was he who reminded me that an organ requires an organist. Ernest is an organ builder; not only has he written books about organs, but he can find his way blindfolded and unerring up five dusty ladders to the smallest piccolo pipe. "*You* think," he told me dryly, "that the Lord Himself reaches right down from Heaven on a Sunday morning and pulls out the stops. Well, you come to the factory with me on Monday, and see what has to happen before the Lord intervenes."

None less than an Ernest could persuade me into a factory of any kind, especially if it meant leaving Gilead for as much as a day. Last summer our Gilead farm acquired a piano, and upon hearing of it, Ernest came to visit. During previous summers, he and I had played sonatas upon every piano in the village – Mrs. Martin's and Dr. Douglas's square ones, and Miss Carrie's upright that balks at all music more modern than Scarlatti. Ernest had acquired a Gilead-piano technique, tinkling and musty; to match it I drew always a light bow, soft-speaking and suited to New England parlors with the blinds decorously drawn.

But in the winter somebody's great-aunt died and left us her piano, sight unseen. It came out to the farm on a truck; an old Steinway, beautifully designed, it melted into our Gilead parlor with the ease of its breeding. In my absence a man came and tuned it and did something to the sounding board which appeared upon the bill in very large letters. Shortly thereafter Ernest arrived, dragging from his automobile two large, heavy suitcases. "Whatever did you bring?" I asked, envisioning sartorial splendor. To which he replied, without hesitation, "Mostly Bach, although I have a little Mozart, too" – and hurried before me into the house. Instantly, trees and pastures resounded with the precise and vigorous opening chords of the "E Major Sonata," but before I could fairly tune my fiddle Ernest had stopped playing. Muttering, he rose and leaned over the opened piano. He pulled out the keyboard and, inquiring bitterly what that man thought he had done for twenty-five dollars, dove into the instrument, wrenched out its bowels, and spread them on the floor.

During the ensuing two hours I learned more about pianos than I had known in thirty-six years;

I learned also about Ernest and about organists in general. Subsequently I have found that craftsmanship is a characteristic of organists; perhaps this is what makes them, as musicians, so reassuring, so convincing. Pleasant to sail great waters with a man who not only manœuvres gracefully in the race, but who can, on occasion, beach and calk a leaky boat. But like all excellence, Ernest's perfection of musical competence demands – and justly – its price, demands of its companions a like competence. To knowledge, ignorance is anything but amusing. Watching Ernest replace the Steinway viscera, hearing each key ring softly into place where before had been mush or silence, I was ashamed that I could not so much as adjust, on occasion, a fallen fiddle sound-post.

Filled with zeal and humility, I followed Ernest to the organ factory. Driving to town, he asked if I objected to curly-haired men? Familiar with New England roundabout habits of speech, I merely inquired, as reply, what curly-haired man Ernest did *not* like, and why?

"Oh, I don't dis*like* Benson," Ernest replied. "He 's the salesman who will show us round to-day. He 's what he 's meant to be. He 's not an organ builder. He 's not a craftsman. He 's a go-getter. If you call him that to his face, he 'll like it."

Ernest steered my ancient flivver expertly through summer-dried Rhode Island ruts. We entered the city, and heat simmered up from melted asphalt. "But," he continued, "if a person 's out to learn about organs, she might as well be partisan. She might as well line up with the true faith."

For two hours I followed Ernest and the curly head from cellar to attic, from pipe to pipe. In the attic the wall thermometer said ninety-six degrees, in the cellar a mere ninety-two. Neither Ernest nor the salesman appeared to notice it; the one talked continuously, rapidly, with enthusiasm and with gestures, while the other, after the manner of experts and scholars, listened gravely, punctuating with an occasional curt remark which brought the flow to a full stop. "You are right," the salesman would agree with a sigh, and would swallow and proceed to other points. Everywhere were pipes, boxed and unboxed; against the walls leaned great wooden diapasons, thirty-two feet high. "Once," said the salesman, "we were installing an organ in the First Baptist Church and one of our salesmen stepped on the bung of a sixteen-foot pipe and fell down inside. Slowed us up considerably, having to fish him out."

A small pipe was handed me. "Blow on it,"

said the salesman. . . . "Now blow this one. . . . Which do you like? . . . A bit fluty, the first one? Tone a little dark, eh?"

They were, to me, identical, and I said so. Ernest shook his head, the salesman was surprised, apologetic. He had thought I, too, was an organist. A mere fiddler, I had discovered, has no ears to hear. We went into the erecting room and on a testing console the men pulled out various stops, arguing vigorously. Tones which to me were merely clear and pleasing to them were bright, dark, spiky, stringy, muddy. "What a grand new language!" I told the salesman. "And how vividly you use it!"

The salesman beamed, but Ernest's lip curled. "Literary terms are both unreliable and unprofitable when applied to sound. It 's a matter of physical vibrations, of primary and secondary partials."

"Smack me down as you will, Ernest," I replied cheerfully. "Until to-day I never knew that any ears, excepting the ears of famous orchestral conductors, could function as yours and this gentleman's can function."

The gentleman interpolated modestly that I could n't have been around much, and told a story about installing the celebrated organ at St. George's

Hall in Liverpool. Working long hours, the men were tired, edgy. "Old Mr. Willis," said the salesman, "signaled for a pipe to be made louder. 'Just a thought!' Old Willis shouted. The man inside the organ had had enough, and anyway he knew the boss was splitting hairs. So he took the pipe out of its rack and put it back without changing the regulation. 'Overdone!' shouts Old Willis. 'But I did n't touch it, sir,' says the workman, and Old Willis shouts back, 'Then why the hell did n't you?' "

The three of us walked on, treading upon sawdust, breathing sawdust. I understood now why Mr. Lamb, for fifty years archdean and king of English organ makers, never rises from a chair or leaves a room – no matter what tapestried chair, what pleasure parlors – without the decisive motion of brushing sawdust from his backside.

Here in this place, men could not only hear, they could feel. Finger tips as well as ears were delicately sentient. A gray-haired man sitting on a high stool bent over a tiny brass reed-tongue in his hand; he rubbed the reed with a burnisher, sighted it, and burnished it again. He was, he told me, curving the tongue of a *tromba* pipe; no machine, no mechanical contrivance, could gauge the proper curvature. His obvious pride and pleasure in his skill filled me also with pride, silencing for once the familiar lament that our world is machine-ridden, mechanized to desiccation. Later, in the ninety-six-degree attic, I was introduced to the boss, the man who had built this famous factory thirty years ago. I saw him at the end of a long room, a tall man, white-haired, without coat or collar. What he was doing I have no idea, but he leaned over a high table, grasping it with his hands; his right foot was hard down on what looked like a pedal, and his left extended in the air behind him. Was this the man who had been described to me as the possessor of foreign-made limousines and marble swimming pools? Absently, but with courtesy, he permitted an introduction, shook hands, and was instantly back upon the pedal. I knew a sudden uprush within, an added glow that had nothing to do with degrees Fahrenheit.

"Ernest!" I whispered. "It 's real pride in craftsmanship. It 's grand. It 's mediæval!"

Ernest looked gratified, but caught himself, and frowned. Ernest does not hold with romanticizing. "It 's not mediæval," he said. "It 's just good organ building."

Driving home through long, elm-shadowed roads, I told Ernest he had been too severe on the salesman. "I liked him," I said. "He was so enthusiastic."

"Enthusiastic?" Ernest sniffed. "Who wants anybody to be enthusi*as*tic?" His tone was acid. "Enthusiasm! What kind of a trait is that? Blind, fudgy business! Nothing behind it, nothing beyond it – "

We lurched round our home curve by the barley field, up our home hill. Dogs barked, children shouted a welcome. "I had hoped you would learn something, to-day," said Ernest sadly, climbing from the car. "Enthusiasm? – Bah! Women are all alike."

It was not until much later that I learned what he meant – learned the difference between enthusiasm and the true faith. Ernest taught me – but not until my education had progressed to the point of understanding.

In the organ world, as in any world, there are camps and divisions, wars and cleavages, and the sharpest of these is the cleavage between the organ as sacred and the organ as profane. This is not to say that church organists are religious men; merely that church and concert hall present the instrument in highly differentiated form. Inclination and the nature of his livelihood fix Ernest upon the ecclesiastical side. Inclination is hardly the word – we could not so much as drive to Willimantic for the weekly groceries without examining at least two organs en route. Impossible for Ernest to pass a country steeple without stopping, and his way with janitors is a triumph of tact.

I would sit in the empty church while Ernest ascended the choir loft. Ernest has an uncanny instinct for the location of keys to locked organs; I would hear him muttering to himself, lids opening and closing, and then a clacking would begin. The clacking, I soon learned, was the loosened parts of the old instrument. "Just ignore it," said Ernest. Then a long sound, silvery and clear. "That 's a nice diapason chorus," Ernest would call. "Don't you like these old Johnson organs? Listen to the flutes, now – "

It was apropos of church organs and craftsmanship that Ernest told me about blessing the organ at Trinity College Chapel. It must have stuck in Ernest's craw, my remark at the factory. "Mediæval," he repeated one day when we were organ exploring around Gilead. "Well, perhaps – "

It seems that during the building of the Trinity Chapel, regular services were held for the workmen every week. When the time came to install the new organ, the men from the Skinner Company asked if they could have a special service for the blessing of the instrument. "It was quite an occasion," said Ernest. Boxes were piled in the Chapel, half unpacked; all around the walls, great pipes leaned. The president of the college, resplendent in brilliant cope, led the service with his two little sons as acolytes. The workmen presented a metal flute pipe for inspection; the president handed it to the little boys, each of whom proved it with a toot. With a censer the president then blessed all the organ parts and the builders.

Fishing in his music case on the car floor, Ernest produced a printed sheet. It was an account of the formal consecration of the Chapel itself: —

At the time appointed for the consecration, the specially invited guests will be in their seats in the Chapel. Professor Merritt will be on the organ bench, the organ being silent; with him will be the donor of the organ, the builder of the organ, Mr. Harrison, the college organist for next year, and Dr. Tertius Noble. John Saul, foreman of the organ workmen, will be in the organ loft. The bells will also be silent, with the visiting *carillonneur* in the bell tower. Inside the closed doors of the Chapel will be gathered the Chapel workmen, with the donor, the contractors, the architects, the college engineer, the artist of the glass, and the artist of the carven wood.

I gave an exclamation of delight. "Wait till you hear the foreman's name," Ernest said. He took the paper from me and read aloud: —

The North Chapel Procession passes directly into the Chapel of the Perfect Friendship, where Angelo Paternostro, foreman of the laborers, is in charge. Led by the crucifer, the president with the thurifer shall conduct the consecrating Bishop to the crossing. There they will halt and the Bishop shall turn to the organ and bless it in this wise: —

"O Eternal God, bless, we pray Thee, this instrument of music, wherein the craftsmanship of many hands has been combined for Thy greater glory. May its subtle melodies uplift the weary soul, may its sturdy chords strengthen the vacillating will, and may its crashing harmonies serve to accompany the voices of those who in this place would hymn Thy praise, who livest and reignest, Father, Son, and Holy Spirit, world without end, Amen."

The president shall then bid the organ sound forth, saying: —

"O all ye works of the Lord, bless ye the Lord, praise Him and magnify Him forever. O all ye wood and metal, bless ye the Lord; O all ye leather and rubber, bless ye the Lord; O all ye electric wires and cunningly devised gadgets . . ."

"Ernest!" I cried. "I don't believe it. You are making it up as you go along."

Ernest pushed the paper before me and read on: —

"O all ye electric wires and cunningly devised gadgets, bless ye the Lord, praise Him and magnify Him forever.

"Praise Him in the sound of the trumpet: praise Him upon the lute and harp.

"Praise Him upon the well-tuned cymbals: praise Him upon the loud cymbals, and upon the strings and pipe."

Ernest released the brake and my flivver slid into gear down Windham Hill. "Let everything," we chanted as we rolled over the blowing shadows of clouds, over the shadows of maple trees and of tall corn lining the road's edge, "let everything that hath breath praise the Lord."

A month after Ernest had left the farm, I found myself in Boston with a whole day to my credit, to spend as I pleased. Over the telephone Ernest instructed me to meet him at the University Chapel at noon. With time out for lunch and for an excursion to the organ loft, we sat upon that organ bench until six o'clock, or Ernest did. My own inferior anatomy rebelled, and I retreated from time to time to the cushioned choir pews or stood on my two feet, but drawn back always to the bench to watch, fascinated, Ernest's hands upon the stops, to answer his challenge – "How do you like *this* combination?"

"What wonderful names for cows, Ernest!" I said. "Dulciana and Celeste. Gamba and Lieblich Gedeckt – ".

In the choir room was a bottle of port, – which Ernest, dispensing hospitality, told me organists usually keep in the organ, for emergencies, – and a shelf of books. I read the titles aloud. "*Tale of a Tub; Portrait of a Lady; Canterbury Tales; Reason in Art; Oxford Book of Ballads; Oxford Book of English Verse*. . . . Very nice," I said, "but what has this to do with organ playing?"

Ernest replied that it had a great deal to do with organ playing. Any one of these books, propped on the music rack, would carry an organist through a bad Sunday sermon. . . .

The D pipe, it seems, would not speak. Flinging off his coat, Ernest sprang aloft like a sailor and I blundered after him. All organists are agile; scrambling after this one, squeezing myself between a forest of dusty diapasons, I wondered. What would happen if Ernest were to get fat? If any organist were to get fat? The D pipe would have to remain silent until a thin tuner could be called. I began to understand how an organ could cost fifty thousand dollars. Ernest told me of more than one parson who thought organ builders were pirates until he saw the parts arriving, truckload upon truckload. Leaning against the wall, his hand on the reservoir as on the shoulder of a friend, Ernest warmed to his theme; I had never heard him talk so easily. "At last," I wanted to say, "Ernest, I see you at home." But I did not dare. He was telling me about the organist who from inside the Wanamaker instrument, on a tuning keyboard, improvised counterpoint on a ribald theme while the regular organist was giving a recital. Profanely reared as I have been, I was on the point of asking what *was* a ribald musical theme, when Ernest, taking from its rack a tiny delicate pipe, blew an octave above high C. "It 's a sound," I said. "But if it 's a note, I 'm as deaf as I was to those bass octaves."

Ernest had no quarrel with my statement. "When this organ was only half tuned," he continued, "they began to use the building for daily service. Every morning after chapel, the tuners set to work. The foreman was a high-strung, irritable Frenchman. Everyone working under him took terrible punishment and wished him repeatedly in hell, where he belonged. One morning in chapel the Dean was casting round for a moral illustration; he cited Pierre as a man who heard dissonances which the ordinary ear could n't recognize. 'So it is,' said the Dean, 'with holiness and the saints.' "

Ernest shook his head. "The pulpit was never more successfully ironic." Absently he took down a square wooden pipe marked "Lieblich Bourdon," blew it, took down another, blew them together, and the Market Street Ferry leaped hoarsely from its slip. "Make you homesick for Philadelphia?" said Ernest.

Ignoring this, I inquired who was the best workman he had known, and Ernest replied instantly, "Old Fleming. At the Wanamaker shop." Old Fleming, it seems, hated the clergy, said all religion was poppycock, was the first man at the shop in the morning and the last one out at night, worked daily until he was seventy-five, delighted to take infinite pains in designing original action, swore like a buccaneer, never fired a workman, but made life so miserable for the incompetent that they had to quit or go crazy, and always wore a white necktie. . . .

I interrupted. "One of the most effective disguises for sin. I have known three equally successful sinners who always wore white ties."

Ernest looked at me darkly and inquired what did it matter, what ties Old Fleming had worn? "He was a superb craftsman who always used five screws where four would do."

"An epitaph, Ernest!" I cried. "Shall we carve it on your tombstone, too?"

Ernest sneezed, brushed dust from his elbows, and preceded me down the ladder. We returned to the organ bench and to Bach. He would now show me, said he, what an organ should *not* do. Tremolo, for instance – which could never, by the very laws of organ structure, equal an orchestral tremolo – should be used sparingly. Chimes were only a sop to the gallery and had better be left out entirely. As to the practice of putting a piano inside an organ, and drums and a xylophone! Ernest shrugged.

As he talked – more to himself than to me – I began to see that what he was expounding would apply to a larger musical area than the organ. To all the arts, indeed. It was the classic principle as opposed to the romantic; what Ernest wanted of his instrument was clear precision – nothing "dark" or throaty, oversensuous or overlanguid. "The eighteenth-century builders," he told me, "made the organ a perfect instrument for contrapuntal music. There is no room in a Bach fugue for blurring and mooning and wooshing *crescendo* on the *gross flute*."

He spoke without haste, but not without intensity. "Solo voices, gorgeous solo stops, are all very well if kept in their place. But they should never be developed at the expense of the ensemble."

The true faith. . . . "Written on my heart, Ernest!" I cried, and there was again heat in Ernest's voice as he continued: "An organ is not a stunt maker. It is an organ, and should be used as such. Its tone is inert. There is not a pipe on the sound board capable of a tone such as you can make with one stroke of your fiddle bow. *But,* it has that other thing – it has brilliance, the finest extreme of exhilaration."

"In other words," said I, glibly, "like all instruments, – like man himself, – your organ is truly effective only when its limitations have been learned and accepted."

A cold, familiar gleam came into Ernest's eye, and I quailed. With Ernest, it is unsafe to be either trite or sententious. But to-day he was too filled with his subject to be diverted into minor annihilations. "If you had your fiddle here, I would show you what I mean." He took a key from his pocket and prepared to lock up his instrument for the night. "What possessed you," he said, "coming to town for a whole day without your violin?"

In the autumn, when I returned to Philadelphia, I was surprised to find myself habitually investigating organs as though it were my business. Driving alone from suburb to suburb, from church to church, blundering in at the wrong doors, groping my way through bleak Sunday School rooms to the organ console, I asked myself: Why should a mere fiddler have become, in the horrid phrase of salesmanship, organ-conscious? Would it prove vicious, this organ habit Ernest had formed in me? If knowledge meant the reaching of conclusions, certainly I was no nearer organ knowledge than I had been in Antwerp Cathedral. Amid these forests of pipes, great and small, amid these choruses and choirs and diapasons, I was lost completely, yet such was the fascination of the siren voices that I was unready to return home even had I known the way.

One Tuesday night I found myself telling my string quartet that this minuet we were playing would sound well on the organ. Dr. Retinus looked at me in amazement. "What has come over you?" he asked. "An organ is all right for processionals and preludes, for roarings and liturgical whoopings. But a minuet? Great clumsy howling business – "

"She has seen the elephants dance," said Henry Jones, sadly, settling his cello peg in the hole reserved for it, "and she will never be the same again." He looked at me gravely. "I, Kala Nag, salute thee, Mowgli." And, craning his head forward, he opened his mouth and gave vent to a long and deafening pachydermal scream.

"How about theatre organs?" said Joe Knoedler, as soon as he could speak. "They play dance music. Whether it 's good or bad, half America hears it. In fact, it 's the only first-hand music half America does hear. Why don't you investigate *that?*"

"She won't like it," said Dr. Retinus. "It 's all nonsense. She 'd better stay where she belongs."

"Women never stay where they belong," Henry Jones said gloomily.

Either of these remarks, I thought afterward, was enough to impel any self-respecting woman up the fence and over into strange territory. It was strange territory indeed, where I found myself upon the following Friday afternoon – on the twentieth row, extreme left-hand end seat, of the largest theatre in the world, waiting for Mr. Sellers to come out and play his organ. The longer I waited, the more uneasily I wondered if Dr. Retinus could possibly have been right. . . .

I looked up. Over my shoulder, somebody was undoubtedly arriving; my dazzled eye told me that whoever it was was bringing his platform with him. It was Mr. Sellers, sure enough, spotlighted at the organ console, sailing triumphantly out from the wings.

I must have made an exclamation, for the woman

on my right leaned to me. "He presses a button," she whispered, "and the organ brings him in."

"Oh!" I said.

Above my head, castanets clicked, a piano trilled, shattering into brilliant pianistic runs. Drums beat a light, uneven rhythm. "It 's a Spanish number," volunteered my neighbor, hoarsely. "He's playing a Spanish piece."

"Oh!" I said again. Bells were ringing, chimes fell in slow cascade. . . . Would that, now, be the Spanish convent? . . . Click clack, click clack – the elephants were dancing. Spanish elephants, maybe? I began to feel more confused than ever. Organ? It was a lot of things, but who said it was an organ . . .

Suddenly, there was clapping. Was that inside the pipes, too? It was not. The audience, some three thousand strong, *liked* the Spanish number; they liked it enough for three Sellers bows in the spotlight. What a pleasant-looking man, I thought, clapping too. Young, and so vigorous. Bouncing up, bouncing down. Curly golden hair, smiling blue eyes. And then, suddenly, nothing. No bouncing. No organ, no golden hair. Only a waving curtain. Evidently Mr. Sellers had pushed another button.

Against what Dr. Retinus would no doubt have

called my better judgment, I went backstage and met Mr. Sellers. I had an appointment to meet him. "How did you like it?" he asked instantly, and while I fumbled with the wrong words, he found the right ones for me. *Not* castanets. A tambourine, that had been. They liked tambourines, out there in front. They liked all the tricks, and he *knew* the tricks. And right now, I might as well know where he stood, said Mr. Sellers. He hated Bach and he hated church organs. The organ was a concert instrument, a solo instrument, an instrument for the virtuoso. Yes, it was true he had won his way through one of the best conservatories in the country; it was true the Mammoth Theatre paid him that mammoth sum per annum as advertised, even if this organ had *not* cost a hundred and fifty thousand dollars. Yes, he had often played at St. Patrick's on the Avenue and could step in and pick up the liturgical service from the Vatican when the wave length broke. It was true also that he had studied with Pietro Yon, who possessed, said he, the cleverest system for galloping from C to A on the pedals ever devised by man.

"But," said Mr. Sellers, "I want you to know where I stand. . . . Bach?"

He threw up his hands. "On and on and on.

Fugues and fantasies. It 's boring. It 's horrible."

Mr. Sellers, it was becoming clear, did not like Bach. It was becoming even clearer, though far less important, that I was not going to like Mr. Sellers.

"Here 's where I stand!" He leaned toward me, hands in pockets. The blue eyes snapped. "I 'm not a musician and I don't want to be called a musician. I 'm a showman."

Relief surged through me. My antagonism for his music would never go, but my antagonism for Mr. Sellers was gone forever, with his last words. Here was a man who knew what he was and what he wanted. I told him so, inquiring bluntly what *were* his standards, musically? With his thumb – but not without respect – Mr. Sellers indicated the vast thousands beyond the curtain. "I go out there and I play. If they like it, it 's good art; if they don't, it 's bad art. And let me tell you, if it 's bad, I know it very, very definitely – and I know it twice. First from my audience, and then from headquarters. There 's no fooling in this business."

Once more I agreed, adding – a little gratuitously perhaps – that I was sorry he found it necessary to be so much on the defensive about Bach. Because –

"On the defensive?" Mr. Sellers shook his head decisively. He was not on the defensive about Bach; he was on the *aggressive,* the same as he was about all this long-drawn-out classical music. He was on the aggressive also when I suggested an excursion into the organ loft. "God, no!" he said. "All those dirty pipes? – I went inside an organ once. *Just* once. I nearly choked to death. Dust. Grime. I 'm not interested in organ building. When a pipe does n't speak, I call the tuner on the phone."

"You press a button," I said. I could not help but say it.

Mr. Sellers grinned; his grin was contagious in the extreme. "I press a button. I 'm not a musician and I'm not a mechanic. . . . Listen! I 'm a – "

"Showman!" I shouted.

Mr. Sellers reached out and, grasping my hand, shook it cordially. "We could get along," he said. "I did n't think so at first, but we could get along."

I agreed with him heartily, on both counts. And if he would come to Philadelphia some Sunday afternoon, my brother John and I would show him – I *bet* we could show him – some Bach that would not bore him.

Mr. Sellers made it instantly clear that no imagined purgatory could possibly equal the coincidence of Philadelphia and Sunday afternoon. Even without Bach. I was the more gratified therefore when, in parting, he inquired, *What* Sunday? – and wrote it down in a little book.

All the way home in the train, I planned what we would sing on that far Sunday. And all the way home I puzzled about Mr. Sellers, his musical origin and history. He had mentioned the name of Yon as teacher. Pietro Yon, the world's greatest organ virtuoso. How could a Sellers have stemmed from a Pietro Yon? Bach? But Bach was bread to Pietro Yon, and more than bread. Years ago, I had wandered into St. Patrick's and heard Yon play the organ; I had even met him afterward and talked with him a little. Strange, that for years I could have forgotten so completely that interview! Even while organ exploring with Ernest, the Yon episode had not returned to me and I had never so much as mentioned his name to Ernest. But it returned to me now, and with force. . . . Mr. Sellers had called himself a showman and in defense had added, "Pietro Yon, he 's a showman too." . . . *"I wear always two flags,"* Mr. Yon had said to me, standing in the half-light of the Cathedral nave. I remembered his brown eyes, set so neatly in his face, bright, intent – "I wear always two flags.

One for the Church, one for the concert hall. When I play in concert, *I* am the picture. But when I play here, in the Cathedral, I am only the frame. There, *there* is the picture."

He had turned his eye eastward, to the altar, and in the upward motion of his hand had been no hint of showmanship. "Bach?" he had repeated after me. "But I can fill Carnegie Hall for a Bach programme. I have made the Indians like Bach. In Oklahoma I missed my train, playing Bach for the Indians."

He had gone on to explain that to make a fugue interesting was a matter of phrasing. One must phrase the theme, not only the first time it appeared, but every time, in every voice. He had smiled. "With five voices, there will be five times the fascination – "

And from this source Mr. Sellers had sprung. Not only sprung, but had the intention of returning for more study. He had told me so. Well, and for all I knew Mr. Edgar Guest had once learned metrics under William Butler Yeats. . . . But what should we sing, on Sunday the twentieth?

John and Sarah rose instantly to the challenge. The "Magnificat," John said. He'd like to see anybody who could hold out against *that*. I agreed. "And would you mind," I said, "singing something with me now, this minute? Get David and Cynthia in from the dining room."

"Something special you want to try?" John asked. "Bach?"

I nodded. Cynthia came down the steps, and David and the others. I wished that it were not so late; I should have liked to invite Dr. Retinus and Henry Jones as witness to this performance. I was about to make public confession. This day I had, indeed, ventured where I did not belong; I, who was fashioned to walk in bright classic pastures, had blustered into the dark throbbing forests of Brobdingnag, and had not come out unscarred. Hereafter I should stay gladly, and in spite of prophecy, where I belonged. . . .

I placed some music on the piano rack. "Here 's what I want to sing," I said. And John said: —

"Good. *Good!* Come on, now . . . David, see if you can double with somebody on the alto chorale. I 'll take the tenor. . . . One, two — "

"Fare thee well, transgression . . ."

CHAPTER XII

A little evening of music, or how not to do it, with a few remarks, highly colored, highly prejudiced, and not a little cocksure, on audiences

ANYONE who plays an instrument acceptably has endured numberless surprise musical parties – given in the player's honor or for reasons equally strange. I went upon a summer week-end to visit Miss Lydia, whom I adore. In her pleasant music room we played Schubert, while beyond the window ships called to each other in a brisk New England harbor. . . . Miss Lydia plays the "D Major Sonatina" in a fashion all her own, a fashion that has not been heard upon this planet since the eighteen-nineties. Delicately, waltzily, with little leapings of the hands and an enormous concentration. On tiptoe we bounded from measure to measure. "Oh, dear," she sighed now and again. "Oh, dear," but she did not stop. Always gallant, with the courage of your true lady, she went bravely, daintily, to the last chord, the last resolution.

"I used to practise very hard when I was young," she told me – and it was true. For all her lavender-and-tea-rose atmosphere, Miss Lydia was the first woman to receive, a long time ago, the degree of Doctor of Music from Yale. "But," she went on, "it is a great many years since I have worked. Do you really think I could play the Schubert better a second time?"

"People do," I assured her cheerfully; a preacher would undoubtedly have added, "That is what second times are for." And third times. "To-night," I told her, "we will play the 'D Major' again, and then the 'A Minor.'"

Miss Lydia made no reply; her expression was strange. Why, I inquired, did she look suddenly as if she had been caught stealing jam?

She asked if I had forgotten Lief Sorenson, who was coming to-night to play Beethoven with me, and I replied that I was looking forward to meeting Mr. Sorenson, but there would be time also for Miss Lydia and Schubert. "You and Miss Polly can sit over there by those roses and that small coal fire, and listen while Sorenson and I do Beethoven. We will lock the doors and stifle the telephone and make an evening of it. I can wear old, comfortable violin clothes and Sorenson can take his coat off. We will play all the rondos and minuets twice over and we will count the *andantes* out loud when they go into sixty-fourth notes. And then you and I will try the Schubert, and Sorenson can tell us what is wrong with the way we do it."

Miss Lydia got up, and sat down again. "A few people are coming," she said faintly. "This town has so little music. . . . It seemed foolish for my sister and me to keep you all to ourselves. . . . So I just invited – "

She reached in a handkerchief bag and produced a slip of paper. List of guests. She said perhaps I had better put away my violin and sit there, quietly, while she told me who was coming? "You have," she finished, "a dangerous propensity for the wrong names at parties, particularly when the person is important."

I rose to my feet and bombed Miss Lydia with loud, explosive words – *betrayal, faithless friend.* She had lured us, me and my fiddle, to this remote and fashionable town by promising us a young pianist who understood Beethoven. She had promised music; did she think a musical evening a fair – even a remotely fair – substitute? Ladies sitting prettily on sofas, men creaking their shirt fronts in anguish through the cadenzas. . . . Fiercely I demanded her real reason for filling the room with people that did n't care for music anyway, asked her why ladies with houses *always* filled the houses with people that did n't care for music. . . .

Miss Lydia was indignant. She said these people *did* care for music. She had invited only—her brow crinkled—fifteen people, and they all *loved* music. That, she assured me, was why she had asked them. Here was I, and my violin, and here was young Mr. Sorenson who played so beautifully on the piano, and why, she inquired again, should Polly and she be so mean as to keep all that to themselves?

I groaned. I told Miss Lydia I had heard that argument, that splendid altruistic poem, ten hundred and fifty-six times in my life; that as poem it was perhaps pretty, but as argument it was thin with holes and I did not trust a word of it. Miss Lydia flushed a little and sat up very straight. "Miss Crittendon is coming," she began. This was, it seemed, the Sarah Crittendon who used to play the piano; an inveterate concert-goer. Of *course* she loved music. Lavinia Doodlespink was coming with her.

I remarked bitterly that I supposed Lavinia used to play the piano, too? And Miss Lydia, ignoring me, went on to say that Lavinia had the most beautiful music room in Boston. Enormous, with perfect Flemish tapestries and a vaulted ceiling. "You go down three steps," said Miss Lydia with enthusiasm –

I said, Oh no, I did n't. Not if it had a vaulted ceiling. I had played to too many echoes in my day. I was about to add that yodeling cellars were all very well in the Alps, when Miss Lydia, her voice a trifle higher, continued the list with the name of Mr. Horace Wimbledon. And his wife. "Of course," said Miss Lydia, "*she* does n't care particularly for music, but she is a charming woman. She has a great deal of money – really a *great* deal of money, and he – "

"Sings!" I shouted. "You don't have to tell me. I know it, from the guilty look on your face. Tenor, I 'll be bound!"

Miss Lydia shook her head. "Not tenor. Barytone." We could, she added confidently, keep him from singing. She knew how to keep him from singing. He used to be a professional singer, – opera, she believed, – and then he married Mary Van Dusen.

"And you think you can keep a maritally suppressed barytone from singing at a party?" I shouted again. "Miss Lydia, if I did not both love and respect you, I should say you were crazy."

I demanded how Mr. Sorenson would like all this – Sorenson, who had been described to me as a professional pianist, and a real musician besides?

Miss Lydia replied with dignity that she was coming to Lief Sorenson in a minute. Lief, she said, was a dear boy – so handsome – and an old friend of hers. "He wants," added Miss Lydia with satanic cunning, "to meet *you.* He likes to play ensemble and has very little opportunity, and he is coming here any minute for rehearsal."

Rehearsal. . . . Horrid word, I thought, redolent of performance, of bracing oneself to please. I sighed again and Miss Lydia went on to say that Dr. and Mrs. Platonic were coming. She could promise that I should like them. I should *really* like them. He was professor of philosophy at the university, and she –

"Used to play the piano?"

Miss Lydia laughed outright and said yes, she still did play it. With her husband – duets on two pianos every evening. "They can be heard," said Miss Lydia, "for blocks."

I said those were the first encouraging words I had heard concerning this party, and I should enjoy very much playing Beethoven for Dr. and Mrs. Platonic. Was anyone else invited who did something with music besides saying he loved it?

Miss Lydia told me I was extremely unreasonable about this. I was, she said, very nearly a fanatic on the subject. Most people have no time to keep up their music. People lead, she said, very busy lives –

Then, I retorted, let them lead their busy lives at home, and not come creaking into nice, fire-lighted music rooms spoiling less busy people's lives.

Miss Lydia turned on me sharply. "You are almost offensive," she said, and began to tell off names upon her fingers. Mr. and Mrs. Beacon Street and their cousins the Back Bays, with their daughter Marina, who was studying at the Conservatory . . .

I said Marina would keep *that* situation in hand, and Miss Lydia went over half a dozen more names, assuring me, almost convincing me, of the genuine desire of their owners to hear Mr. Sorenson and me play Beethoven. Then she said, "And Mrs. Whiting-Roberts" – and stopped.

I said, "Well?" Miss Lydia replied that of course I knew whom she meant? I did not, and Miss Lydia frowned and said I was sometimes a little difficult. Mrs. Whiting-Roberts was – well, she had donated that whole enormous picture gallery I saw on the way up the hill, the one with the marble pillars. She had endowed string quartets and contributed Skinner organs. Everyone in the world knew about Mrs. Whiting-Roberts. She was an old friend of Miss Lydia's before she married Mr. Whiting-Roberts, who had died, by the way, some time ago, and now Anstice had this huge fortune to take care of. So Miss Lydia had invited her to-night in order that she might hear Lief Sorenson play.

A small silence fell, and settled there.

"Does Mrs. Roberts-Whiting," I asked presently, "know anything about music?"

"Mrs. Whiting-Roberts? No . . ." Miss Lydia looked a trifle embarrassed. "She does n't. She donates organs and finances string quartets because of her daughter. Her daughter is very musical. Her daughter is not coming to-night because she is away. But I thought it would be an opportunity for Mr. Sorenson to be heard by somebody important, and I thought you and he playing together like this would be a nice simple way to introduce him." Anstice Whiting-Roberts, added Miss Lydia, was a delightfully friendly person when you really knew her, but she was apt, with strangers, to be a little *stiff*. Not disagreeably stiff, Miss Lydia amended hurriedly. Just a little *shy*. "She has" – Miss Lydia's gaze went off dreamily – "the most gorgeous string of pearls. Very famous large pink pearls."

Another silence. "I see," I said at last. "Oh, I see *everything*. This is to be Mrs. Roberts-Whiting's party – "

"Mrs. Whiting-Roberts – "

"Who has large pink pearls and is so shy. . . . Very well, Miss Lydia, I understand it all now. Sorenson is to be the main sacrifice and I am here to garnish, as it were, the dish. It is a racket, Miss Lydia dear, a plain racket, but to tell you the truth, I do not mind to-night half so much now I know there is a Purpose behind it. If Sorenson really plays well and needs advertisement, I shall be happy, as we say in Philadelphia, to coöperate. Fifteen people who love music and one person who knows nothing of music, but has large pink pearls. . . . That makes sixteen, all coming to our musical party."

The doorbell rang. Into the room bounded a blond young man who smiled, bowed neatly from the hips, sat down at the piano, and struck A. We played the Beethoven "Fourth." The young man smiled again, and I turned to my hostess. "Miss Lydia darling," I said, "for the privilege of playing with Mr. Sorenson, I will do sonatinas for Mrs. Roberts-Whiting all night."

"Mrs. Whiting-Roberts," Miss Lydia said, and sighed.

Mr. Sorenson looked up. "Shall we play a Brahms now?" he asked. "Oh no, not for rehearsal! We could not attempt Brahms to-night with so little preparation. Not for rehearsal – " he smiled. "For fun."

"Miss Lydia, *dearest,*" I said. "Did you hear that? For the sake of this man on the piano bench I will tie Mrs. Whichis-Whatsis's shoe laces to-night, if they come untied. I will hand her cake upon a plate, and I will, if she desires it, show her I can pick up a pencil with my toes."

Miss Lydia beamed. "I knew," she said, "that you and Mr. Sorenson would understand one another."

The guest of honor sat upon the sofa, unsmiling. For no reason at all I took an instant, violent, and childish dislike to her, but Mr. Sorenson, heedless of the pink pearls, – far, far above any pink pearls, – played as one inspired. Beethoven "Violin Sonata Number 4," in A minor. Very fast he took it, but the force of his impetus, the contagion of his rhythmic sense, kept me abreast. For twenty years I had played that sonata, but to-night were uncovered to me treasures that for twenty years had passed by me unrecognized, but which are mine now forever.

And the operatic barytone did not sing – the first time I ever saw a hostess achieve this particular miracle. No doubt about it, these Miss Lydias, adorable rare gentlewomen of the old school, know how to gain their point. Lavender, tea rose – I always suspected this ancient fragrance of a sinister power of anæsthetization. One sniff, and the victim – particularly if he belong to that class which has not, in youth, become naturally immunized to lavender-and-old-lace great-aunties – remains comatose, sunk in a puzzled, helpless lethargy of politeness.

Sorenson behaved perfectly. When we had played he went to the pink pearls, bowed once, and held no further traffic with anybody. He said to me, "It is late, but would you like to come to the chapel and hear my organ, and would Miss Lydia come too?"

Farewells were said, pleasant murmurings of gratitude for music. The pink pearls glowed, for an instant a hand lay in mine. Something in me relaxed; perhaps the lady really was shy? Perhaps she really did like music? Volubly, of a sudden, I replied to her sallies, I called her by name; Miss

Lydia heard me. I said I hoped we could play for her again sometime. . . .

And the three of us, Miss Lydia and Sorenson and I, went out and up an open road to a chapel, where Miss Lydia and I sat alone under high dim arches and a Voice poured round us, quiet, yet full of motion, great with volume as that sea voice below the hill. . . . *Jesu, joy of man's desiring.* . . . Candle flame and shadow and Johann Sebastian praising his God in a song simple and clear as those small flames pointing upward. . . . Why, I asked Miss Lydia, walking homeward, had n't all organists sense enough to play things like that, instead of causing their instruments to growl and sob and scream in meaningless virtuosity? Miss Lydia replied that I was forever demanding talent and then pretending I was arguing for common sense. She unlocked her door and we stepped across a fragrant threshold. She told me I had behaved well to-night, and then she paused and looked at me. "But," she said, "do you realize — I hope you do not realize — that when you bade good-bye to Anstice Whiting-Roberts, you said, very loud and clear, 'Good-bye, Mrs. Roberts-Whiting'?"

"Miss Lydia," I replied, "by the beard of

Brahms, by the holy deafness of Beethoven, by the key of G minor which I love with all my heart — Oh, by my most potent, private oath, *by the four strings upon my fiddle,* I swear — "

Miss Lydia stopped me. "That is enough," she said, and her hand upon mine was dry and warm and light.

As these things are reckoned, Miss Lydia's was an innocent enough musical party, and not unpleasant in its way. Whether it achieved its object, whether the Pearls gave the Pianist a job, I do not know. But I do know that music, like truth, cannot be abused with impunity. Use Beethoven as an excuse for a pay-off party with which to fulfill your social obligations, and Beethoven — or truth — will turn and rend you. I admit the temptation; a musical party, on the face of it, can house a huger number of guests than perhaps any form of private evening entertainment. And the invited, musical or no, will come. Art is, unfortunately, fashionable; music is smart, and in the name of smartness the world will endure much discomfort. Wives especially; at a musical party they can contrive, even when bored literally sick, an expression of polite or startled inquiry. But husbands! Seated next to such a patient masculine sufferer, and observing the look of stony suffering upon his face, I have been tempted to prod him, to poke him with a pin. "Why do you endure this?" I want to cry. Sheep! Rise up! Rebel! Assert your essential manhood! Not only – I want to say – does your suffering communicate itself to me until my ears are, like yours, drawn back in misery, but you make it impossible for me to hear the music. Yet I do not hate you, neighbor; I desire you, not hung, but rescued. Were this, instead of song, a symposium upon modernistic painting or a demonstration in the art of baking oysters, my face would look even more like yours than my misplaced sympathy is causing it now to look. But, fellow citizen, but, fellow man, I would not *go* to a symposium on oyster baking.

Beethoven is smart and no gainsaying it; the fact, like Margaret Fuller's universe, must be accepted, and I cast about for what good may be drawn from so distasteful an admission.

Money in the musician's purse, food in his mouth, a chance for him to be heard and his compositions known. And also, as Victoria has often reminded me, Smartdom is not all silly, and hard, and self-seeking, and invulnerable to beauty. In the parlors of Mrs. de Courcey I have seen converts made, have seen persons who came for idle reasons awakened suddenly and forever to the charm of intimate music intimately heard. . . . I witnessed this, or something like this, upon that Musical Evening I mentioned in an earlier chapter, when Victoria in Poiret laurels caviled at the word "stylish," and her husband, looking into his hat, suggested wistfully that the "best" people do not always write the best music. That evening was an adventure; I might call it an adventure in audience. Nothing definite occurred – only a woman speaking to me and following me and speaking to me again. What she said surprised me greatly, so that, although her words had little moral and perhaps less meaning, I greatly desire to record them.

Mounting marble stairs, I became separated, somehow, from Victoria, and entered the music room alone. Spindly gold chairs, brocaded Empire sofas, were already filled with people, talking softly, waiting for the music to begin. Over beyond the fireplace, between the piano and a long, curtained window, four men, their faces dark above the white of their dress shirts, tuned their instruments, arranged the always inadequate lights of drawing-room recitals.

There was only one chair left and I captured it – I remember it as the first white satin chair I had ever sat in. Low and heavy, it faced the room, not the musicians; I tried vainly to turn it. Thus I sat, facing the audience, the warmth of a coal fire against my neck and shoulders, the musicians behind me, and shut my eyes because so many faces, ranged point-blank against one, were a trifle bewildering. Thirty faces – fifty? I could not see the faces for the gleaming dresses, for the chandelier, crystal, candlelighted, for the white walls, the flowery carpet. Difficult to differentiate these faces, difficult to – as Mr. Lerando would phrase it – sort them out. I was aware that the fortunate owners of the faces had paid twenty-five dollars each for this evening's entertainment; a series of six musical evenings at twenty-five the evening. Rich people never throw their money away. Then Victoria was right and I was wrong; these people knew what they wanted, and what they wanted was good. These faces, so tired, so sharp, or so vacuous – was it only my biased imagination that painted upon each brow, young and old, a look of exhaustion, as though life held no meaning beyond an endless procession of hours to be filled?

This conviction, however false, was strong; it baffled and depressed me; leaning my head against white cushions, I turned my eyes upward. That chandelier, reflecting in a thousand watery prisms a thousand spears of yellow candle flame – how in the name of morning did they get up there to clean it? Men on ladders in the early sunlight, – Park Avenue sunlight, – shirt-sleeved, aproned, men joshing each other in rough subdued voices. . . .

There was a stir near the door. Into the room swept, darted, danced, a woman, tiny, with black straight hair and the quick movements of a bird. It was as though, suddenly, air had blown into this place, air rich and exciting as wine. I leaned to the left and asked somebody in pale blue, "Who is it? Oh, who is it?" And the lady turned slowly and said, "Don't you know? It 's Bori."

Had she said, "It 's Mrs. Smith," it would have made no difference. An eagle had swooped into this satiny nest, bringing with it air from the mountains and the sound of wings. I said, "Look at her! Look at her face! She puts them all out like a light. And yet she 's not really handsome, and she 's so little. What is it? Is it her genius? Is it" – I thought of my aunt's words – "the fight she has fought?"

The blue satin lady turned again to the door; she leaned forward. "I see what you mean," she said. "But – I don't know. Now, you take all my friends' faces. . . . These people here are all my friends." She paused, gesticulating with the awkwardness of a graceful woman suddenly in earnest. "Oh, you must n't think I mean my friends have n't nice faces." Her brow puckered, she looked faintly distressed, as though caught in a disloyalty, faintly bewildered. "They have *lovely* faces. But they have n't got – they 're not – "

Her voice trailed off; she looked as if she were going to cry. The music began; I knew it less from the sound than from the sudden motion of the woman we were watching. As the violins stopped tuning she had sat down abruptly, with the finality and precision of a soldier at command. The man behind her continued to lean over her solicitously, but it was plain that for her he no longer existed. . . . Faces? There was only one, I knew now, the face of this dark woman, alert, held forward a little from her body, listening, humbled, *waiting* – her face, and the four heavy pale faces above the fiddles.

Debussy, they were playing, and Debussy, I thought, should suit well this gathering. With Debussy the butter is not spread too thick, the bread is never seized and torn hungrily to pieces, but is cut into patterns with a thin, delicious extravagance. Then why did not the audience respond, why were the faces so blank?

Debussy, Mozart, and the Bach "Air for the G String." The cello plucked soft, unhurried accompaniment. . . . We got up and trailed long, light dresses out wide doors and across a black and white floor to the dining room. People laughed and talked softly, but with animation. It was a good party. Very good. Even I could see the especial undeniable goodness of this party. Debussy and pheasant *en galantine* and diamonds in long fiery delicate strands. Victoria, across the room, waved to me, smiling. "But, darling," someone protested to someone else, "of course you like Debussy. Or you will, after a while. It would be impossible not to, like not liking Verlaine. If you bring Cyril to Virginia, Sam will mount him. But of *course* I mean it – "

A funny place, I thought, for an eagle, and then suddenly the eagle swept by. Darted by, the small head magnificently poised upon the small neck, the black eyes snapping, fiery. She was talking ten to the dozen, laughing, gesticulating. Behind her fluttered my pale blue lady, sucked, as it were, helplessly in her wake, like one of those rare smooth-winged parrakeets, suddenly cageless, swept into the passage of a larger bird. When the pale blue lady saw me she stopped and came toward me, her long dress brushing the floor. Patently, she had something to say and meant to say it. Her face was troubled, the brow puckered, the blue eyes wide, earnest.

She began to speak; what she said was, I knew, incredible, but she said it. All evening, this canker must have gnawed at her side. Within those pale blue slippers – made to order at God knows what the slipper – those toes must have curled in stiff, uncomfortable constriction.

She began just where she left off early in the evening and left off just where she began: –

"I did n't mean – I hope you did n't think I meant – I mean about my friends' faces. These – people here – are all my friends. I 've grown up with them. I 'm fond of my friends. They really have lovely faces."

She turned her own face for a long moment eagle-ward, and slowly back to me. Her hands fluttered upward helplessly.

"I just meant . . ."

But why, I wondered, driving homeward, does an eagle look so gloriously like an eagle, and a dove so inevitably like a silly dove? Why is a professional a professional and an amateur a . . . I shook my head; it was not the distinction between amateur and professional for which I sought definition, but another distinction. After a fight, a dove is no longer a dove, but a mess. In this business of the arts, rare is the person who can take a beating; the second picture rejected by the local *salon*, the second play hissed off the boards, and your dove retreats to the nest. But, after a beating, and another beating, and another – still to look like an eagle! That, I told myself with confused, after-the-party logic, is what makes a person look like an eagle. The torn breast as medallion, the bloody crest as crown, the undaunted eye searching a fierce horizon for yet another battle . . .

"Doves?" said Victoria. "Never mind doves. Did you have a nice time? Did you like the party?"

I said I did, and heartily.

But being audience is one thing, being – as at Miss Lydia's – part of the programme is one thing, and being hostess, responsible for the evening, is another. Easy enough to criticize a musical party and tear it to pieces in superior scorn – another matter to stand behind and push the party to success! To feel on one's shoulders the heavy bulk of thirty guests waiting for something to be concluded so that something else can begin and be, happily, concluded in its turn – no wonder the

hostess is nervous! What, she wonders, is the recipe for a successful musical evening?

The recipe is twofold: First, the party, even from its conception, should centre around the programme, the music to be played, rather than around the guests to be invited. In fact, I know of but one legitimate reason – outside of organized charity – for giving a musical party. Let me address the reader directly, intimately, in the modern journalistic manner.

If there is a piece of music you desire to hear performed, and it can be found on no concert programme, if there is a Magnificat with which you long to become familiar and no choir will sing it – then give a musical party. Suppose, for instance, you have never heard the two versions of the Brahms "B Major Piano Trio," for piano, cello, and violin. You are aware that this trio, Opus 8, was written before Brahms was twenty-one, and that years later, at the age of fifty-six, Brahms rewrote it entirely. You long to compare the two versions; why not have them played by a professional trio at your house next Sunday evening? The Browns would be interested, and the Joneses; in fact you are conscious immediately of fifteen people who would stand on tiptoe all evening for the privilege of hearing the two versions of this trio played straight through, one after the other. Ask the Smiths, too; they don't know A flat from B natural, but they are intelligent people, filled with a lively curiosity as to the technique, the procedure, of artistic creation in any medium. Like Sidney's wife, the Smiths will likely demand, "And what *is* a fugue?"

On that evening, thirty ears will bear witness to the astounding proof of a composition transformed from the thin romantic charm of youth to the rich vitality of a courageous maturity. Witnessed so intimately, even the untutored ear can sense the difference. Afterward, over the lobster and champagne or the beer and cheese, eighteen tongues will wag – three of them, the musicians'. People will crowd round the fiddle stands. "Tell us, show us, why such-and-such a passage, though so little changed, sounds so much better in the second version." Nothing is more stirring, more inspiring to witness than the miracle of *growth;* even the layman, the very slightly musical, be he, by day, shoe importer or button manufacturer, by night will know a quickening of his pulses before this published, black and white proof of the miracle. . . . Here was a man, this Brahms, this short stout fellow with the cigar, who destroyed twenty string quartets before he published one, who could by his own confession have papered a house with self-rejected manuscript – and whose eye could look upon his own published opus with a merciless, courageous clearness that would tolerate nothing less than complete reconstruction.

All this the musician retails to the button manufacturer, and the button manufacturer, who last Monday, in the face of a hostile Board of Directors, scrapped his old machines in favor of a brand-new model for the manufacture of better buttons, responds with glowing eye. The musicians, accustomed to neglect at parties, – nobody, after the first congratulations, can think of anything to say to them, – the musicians will be enchanted. The host will be proud, the guests excited; I am not inventing this scene, I have witnessed its enaction.

Informality is your second ingredient in the recipe for a musical evening, and informality cannot be acquired artificially. It grows out of your first ingredient, a sincere love of music. But do not attempt, on the other hand, a haphazard, unplanned musical party. This can succeed only when at least half the guests are musical geniuses and good-natured and friends with each other – an unlikely case. The average host and hostess must have their musical evening organized beforehand like an army drill, like a Monday morning at school. It is to be hoped, of course, that the machinery will not creak or the programme be exposed. John says nothing takes so much sweat as the achievement of casualness, informality in a crowd. I have heard his guests remark, "How wonderfully we all sang the 'Gypsy Songs' to-night!" — little reckoning that skilled sopranos, contraltos, et cetera, had been surreptitiously seated next to the worst singers, or that Lydia Bel Cantor's husband, Mr. Toneless, had been lured half an hour ago into the library for bridge with three other doubtful singers.

Before we learned the technique, John and Sarah and I were responsible for several musical evenings of the dreariest. We made the horrid mistake of playing for the company and expecting the company would want to listen. It did not. All evening we had that nightmare sensation of reaching for something, clutching at something which was not there. We failed, not because we played badly, — we played quite well, — but because we played in our own house. There is something peculiarly irritating about being invited to somebody's house and then forced to listen to one's host exhibit his powers, be they musical, acrobatic, or ventriloquistic. No guest enjoys being trapped into applause, or even into a mild and sugary acquiescence.

This is not to say your party should consist only of playing amateurs or of professional musicians. The latter are, in fact, the last persons to invite unless you are very sure of your programme or number among your guests a Pink Pearl, to meet whom would be of advantage to the musicians in question. . . . But, business aside, professional musicians will come to a musical party if there is abundance of good food and drink, if they know they are to meet their friends, or if they are to take an unofficial part in the programme – provided this part is not a solo upon their own instrument. I need not waste words here upon the well-known abuse of seducing artists to dinner and then asking them to play for their pudding. . . . A famous wood-wind player invited to a musical evening sent back the reply, "A music party? Alas, I have no time for music."

One hundred and thirty pounds of boredom quickly multiplies itself in geometrical ratio. I resent this confession, this admission of the power of audience; I should prefer to believe that music is music, whether played for mandarin or musician. Nevertheless it is true that the moment Audience is admitted, the moment Listener takes its seat, it becomes an intrinsic part of the music, influencing enormously both performer and neighbor listener. In this connection, a simple matter which seems to elude the musical hostess is the fact that different music requires different-sized audiences. Most chamber music is of a nature so intimate, a charm so delicate, that its quality is wholly destroyed under the stampede of eighty breathing mortals. Forty persons is the limit for an evening of string quartets; twenty would be preferable. Rows of chairs kill the more fragile forms of chamber music as surely as a fire-engine siren would kill them. On the other hand, I have seen three hundred persons assembled in a private house to hear a soprano sing operatic airs, and the three hundred only added volume to her already overadequate inflation. The accident that I myself abhor that kind of party is of no more significance, I suppose, than the fact that Dr. Retinus, next to me, sat all evening with his head in his hands, muttering, in the vocabulary of a fiddler, "She needs rosin. For God's sake bring the rosin." Two hundred and ninety-eight persons applauded until the singer melted massively into encores — Old English ditties, coy and lilting, of the "Oh, no, John" variety. The applause of two hundred and ninety-eight is not, I suppose, to be discounted.

But I hoped, as I shuffled slowly upstairs for my coat with those other hundreds when the evening was ended — I hoped only that my hostess did not call what had happened by the name of music.

CHAPTER XIII

And when I shall be old —

In a country town in upper New York State I knew a man, a jeweler by trade, who played the flute until he got so old his lip cracked. Then he set to work and learned the violin, which he played until he died at eighty-four. Once, in his seventies, he fell sick and was bedridden a long time, but nobody was sorry for him. Nobody whispered, "Poor old thing, sitting there all day. Hopeless to try to amuse him, and anyway, we are all too young and busy." Nobody had a chance to patronize Mr. Greening. Because all the time he was in bed, he was busy making violins. He made two, and when he got up he played upon them — both at once, for all I know. He would have been capable of it. One day some callers came — how pitifully most old people are dependent upon the graciousness of an occasional visitor! Not so Mr. Greening, with music for a friend. He endured all this chitchat, he told me afterward, as long as he could, and then, calling his daughter into the parlor, fled upstairs to the bathroom, turned on the water in the tub, and practised.

In America, it is the habit of the young to patronize the old. I do not know why this is so, but I see it all around me, and it fills me with rage and sorrow. In comfortable middle- and upper-class homes, there seems to be nothing for the old to do; not permitted to participate in simple household tasks, they sit – old men especially – and eat their hearts out in querulous discontent or sink into a premature senility that could have been long delayed had they been occupied, urged to use what brain and muscle remained to them. Their middle-aged protectors hover – stout busy harpies – in smothering kindness or frank neglect, waiting for the old to die and make more room for themselves.

And never tell me the old do not know it. The pity is, this humiliation has caught them unaware; fifty years ago, age was respected, even feared. Bridgeless chasms have opened between the generations, and few there be with voices penetrating enough to be heard on the other side. We stand marooned, except for our contemporaries – and with the old, who have lost their contemporaries, that means a truly helpless abandonment. . . . Our parents could not prepare for this, but we can.

We who see the situation, who pride ourselves upon our hard-headed acceptance of fact; we who name the ingratitude of children no sin, but merely one more shell on the already hard-boiled human egg – we have no excuse if we do not prepare for old age. We know we shall be abandoned, – fed, cared for, and abandoned, – and it should be our part to prepare now our defenses.

Already I am preparing mine, and the greatest of these shall be music. Not music as I have it now, but music suited in a practical way to what I can reasonably foretell will be my lot as an old woman. I can expect, for instance, to have very little money, and money is the prime defense, the stiffest rampart, of the aged. Old people with money can always find what passes for a friend. But if I shall have little money, I can hope, observing my parents at eighty-odd, for sight and hearing unimpaired, arteries fairly flexible, and a spirit too bumptious to be quashed at the convenience of my children. Victoria has often tried to put my mother into a lace cap. "On your white hair, darling, it would be lovely. So distinguished – and smart, too." Twice she even manœuvred the cap into position, and the effect, artistically, was enough to melt the heart. But my mother would have none of it; the instant Victoria's train whistled, departing for New York, that lace cap and fichu went back into Grandmother's trunk, and the red silk scarf flashed once more on the maternal shoulders. "I am too spry for my own good," said my mother, surveying herself in the glass. "I give my children much trouble. . . ."

I have observed that old people are more acceptable in a household if they can spend a large part of their time alone, without complaint, happily. I count upon my fingers those septuagenarians who play upon their fiddles alone of an evening, and it shakes me a little to find among them no females! I know more than one grandmother who plays the piano and enjoys duets with the third generation; can it be that a fiddle is too heavy for the grandmotherly shoulder, and must I, at seventy, begin to polish up my pianistic scales? My Tuesday-night string quartet has sworn to play together until its members cease to breathe—three of us, that is. Joe Knoedler is younger by ten years than the others; we know that in spite of his promises he will some day desert our palsied ranks for ensemble more worthy of his strength. Shall I, at seventy-five, be able to substitute, or shall I have forgotten the viola clef? Will that long bow sweep too wide for my rheumatic elbow? That C string, whose delicious shudder even now causes my jaw to vibrate, will it rattle my teeth out entirely? Perhaps I have never mentioned in these pages the fact that I play viola? I learned the instrument two years ago when I saw that Cynthia would soon be premier family fiddler, her younger sister would play second, and where would I be? The viola was my first move in the defensive against old age.

But what lies ahead of me as actual musical participant is, I think, the chair of a good steady second violinist. This is what I hope for. I should be proud of the place; how often I have heard John remark that what America needs is an army of good second fiddlers, and how heartily I agree! But if my hopes are too high, if at seventy or earlier my chin must say a last farewell to that warm fiddle-hardness gripped beneath the jawbone, even then I shall not be defeated. I have a last line of resistance, a great and never-ending resource to fall back upon: I can be listener.

I am preparing myself, now, to be listener. And it requires preparation. I never had a truly musical ear – only a musical emotion and an active brain; it is almost impossible for me to comprehend a piece of difficult music unless I have played it. An enormous literature of music remains to be proved upon my fiddle strings or in my faltering choral throat before I shall be equipped to know it by ear alone! At seventy, I shall begin daily practice in ear training; experience has taught me the value of this practice, but I am too occupied now to include it in the day's programme. I look forward to that far Sunday evening when I shall recognize the diminished fifth as I do my name. . . .

One night recently I went to a concert for which John was responsible, an evening of string quartets in a small hall in town. Beethoven Opus 132 was played, the A minor with the *Heiliger Dankgesang* chorale. Nothing in the literature of classical ensemble is more difficult to perform than the slow movement of this quartet; it requires a sustained emotional intensity that has caused the premature crumpling of many a first violinist. One of the last things Beethoven wrote, filled with the boundless power of his maturity, it is a work of great seriousness. The day before the concert, the musicians had come out to John's house and played it, asking his criticism; John and I had sat, score in hand, marking possible weak places with a pencil. . . .

At the concert the musicians acquitted themselves well; they left the platform looking white, exhausted as though they had met with gloves upon a mat rather than with bows and fiddles upon a polite platform. Behind us sat old Mrs. Van Dusen and her daughter. They leaned toward us. "But what a delightful, jolly piece!" they cried. "We did not dream Beethoven could be so light-minded. Is this one of his earlier, more youthful works?"

"John," I said, when we were out upon the street, "it was n't their fault they could n't understand. Nothing is so difficult to hear for the first time as that 'A Minor Quartet.' Why did n't you stand up and explain it beforehand, tell the people what it was about, what it meant? At least you could have told them about the *Dankgesang* place." John replied gloomily that he would have, but he did n't get out of court until five, and his train was late. When he arrived at the hall the music had already begun. "Well," Sarah said, "I 've heard that quartet all my life, and to-night was the first time I understood it. Oh, what a silly word!" she cried. "*Understood?* – I did n't understand that quartet. It understood me."

"You mean," I suggested, "it 's the first time the 'A Minor' reached out and took you by the hand and made friends with you?"

Sarah looked a little embarrassed. "Maybe," she said, adding that John and I had a creepy way of talking about music.

When I am seventy, I shall begin to go furiously to concerts, all the concerts I can afford – many more than I go to now, occupied as I am with a more active participation in music. I shall keep on going to concerts as long as I can find someone to carry me in and set me down. And I shall make a business of it. When Monday comes, and I am going to a concert Monday evening, I shall save my energy all day, take a long nap in the afternoon so that I shall not, as I now do, sink exhausted in row K and depend upon Beethoven to bring me to life or put me, mercifully, to sleep. It will not require the first three movements of a symphony to clear the daily fog from my brain, to iron out the crazy tangles that bristle now between the innocent ear and the all-too-cautious, all-too-sophisticated cerebellum. No – when I am seventy, if I have not learned, acquired, that peace of soul, that receptivity which is true innocence, then I had rather be dead and worthy of no more various symphony than the rain upon my tombstone.

Thus far, music has been to me something relative. It has been healer, friend, confidant. But when I am old, and have no interesting, remorseful secrets – what will music be then? I do not know, but I have a guess; I have that hint we all receive concerning our future – that extra-curriculum something which the future breathes back to us and which is, in all likelihood, less oracle than the natural prophecy of our blood. Our future is what we ourselves are.

I have a feeling that as my life straightens to level, as the proverbial path becomes less abrupt and the shouting chasms show green meadows — as emotions take a truer proportion, a nicer balance, music, no longer needed as healer, as refuge in storm, will become less of me and more of itself. Music will no longer be Music-and-Me, it will be Music, a thing intrinsic, absolute. I can study it as Euclid studied the circle; I can "see beauty bare." That is my hope, and I trust it is not over-impudent. At thirty-seven I am blinded by the world, busy seeing that the children practise twenty minutes a day, anxious concerning the effect my new dress will have upon my friends. . . . When the wise speak to me of absolutism, of absolute truth, absolute justice, I can no more comprehend than I could comprehend that old physician who spoke to me yesterday so naturally of the "instinct of death." At thirty-seven the fire of life rages so hotly, the "alarum in the breast" beats so loud, so brave, we cannot believe in that last absolutism, death. Everything is relative, everything has the living quality of *dailiness,* and because of these relationships everything – even music – has a thousand approaches, a thousand ways to be conquered.

But some day, not a far day either, I shall perhaps cease conquering, cease being defeated, and I shall begin to accept. And when I have learned to accept, to cease fighting, then I shall have, not more *time* for music, – I have time for it now, – but more room in my soul. When Beethoven comes I shall have, as it were, a house more spacious in which to receive him, not cluttered with the furniture of tears, of ragings, or all noisy with the sounds of my own quarrels with myself.

It is a great, a pleasant thing to have a friend with whom to walk, untroubled, through the woods, by the stream, saying nothing, at peace – the heart all clean and quiet and empty, ready for the spirit that may choose to be its guest.